THE SECRET SIDE OF WEALTH

What the Elite Know About Money, Power, and Freedom and How to Use It to Build Real Wealth

The Hidden Architecture

The path to freedom begins the moment you stop following their map

Table of Contents

Introduction: The Rules You Were Never Taught

Why Wealth Has Always Had a Hidden Side

Wealth has never been a purely financial concept. Throughout history, those who held real power did so not only because they possessed money, but because they understood the unspoken systems that governed its flow. Monarchs, merchants, industrialists, and modern billionaires have all operated within frameworks invisible to most of the population. These frameworks involve networks, influence, timing, and structures that allow wealth to multiply quietly while the majority remain focused on wages and savings.

To understand why this hidden side exists, it is important to look at the dynamics of access and knowledge. Most people are taught a single financial narrative: work hard, save consistently, and eventually retire with security. This message is repeated in schools, traditional financial advice, and even by governments. Yet those who rise to extraordinary levels of wealth follow a very different path. They learn, often through family exposure or elite circles, how to use leverage, tax structures, and insider opportunities that are rarely discussed publicly. This is not because such knowledge is illegal or inaccessible. It is because revealing it broadly would remove the advantage it provides to those already in the know.

The Origins of Hidden Wealth Systems

The idea of concealed wealth strategies is not modern. Ancient merchant guilds in the Mediterranean, for example, built exclusive networks that controlled trade routes and information about prices. In medieval Europe, banking families like the Medicis held extraordinary influence not just through their riches but through their understanding of credit systems and political alliances. They operated in ways invisible to common citizens who relied solely on coins in their pockets.

The industrial revolution magnified this divide. The rise of corporations, stock markets, and modern banking introduced complex mechanisms for building wealth that required specialized knowledge. Industrial magnates did not simply profit from factories; they mastered capital structures, market timing, and insider negotiations that ensured their fortunes grew exponentially while workers earned predictable wages.

Today, the pattern continues in different forms. Technology entrepreneurs and financial elites use tools like equity compensation, venture capital, and tax-efficient trusts that are rarely explained in mainstream financial education. While ordinary people are advised to "get a good job and invest in a retirement account," insiders quietly exploit opportunities that compound wealth at an entirely different pace.

Why This Knowledge Remains Hidden

There is no conspiracy of silence in the sense of a coordinated effort to keep the masses uninformed. Instead, the secrecy comes from complexity and exclusivity. Financial systems are layered, and those layers reward people who already have access. A tax loophole may be openly written into law, but understanding and using it requires resources and advisors beyond the reach of most families. Similarly, opportunities such as early-stage investments are legal but only available to accredited investors who meet certain wealth thresholds.

The result is a cycle where wealth begets knowledge and knowledge begets more wealth. Those who grow up in affluent circles are exposed to conversations and strategies that shape their financial worldview from an early age. They learn how to think about risk differently, how to structure their income, and how to navigate opportunities that seem invisible to outsiders. In contrast, most people are taught simplified rules intended to maintain stability rather than generate extraordinary gains.

Understanding this hidden side is not about resenting those who possess it but about breaking the illusion that everyone plays the same game. Once you see that there are multiple financial games happening simultaneously, you can begin to position yourself differently. This book is designed to bridge that gap, revealing not only what those systems are but also how to start applying their principles in a practical, ethical way.

The Emotional Barrier to Hidden Knowledge

One of the greatest obstacles to uncovering these truths is psychological rather than technical. Many people carry deep-seated beliefs about money shaped by culture, religion, and family history. Ideas like "money is the root of all evil," "rich people are greedy," or "I am just not good with numbers" can act as invisible fences, preventing them from even seeking insider knowledge. Research by psychologists Daniel Kahneman and Amos Tversky in 1979 on loss aversion demonstrated how humans are wired to fear losses more than they value gains. This bias keeps many individuals from taking calculated risks, even when the potential rewards are far greater than the downside.

If you have ever felt hesitant to pursue opportunities that seemed too big or complex, you are not alone. These internal barriers are part of why wealth feels hidden: it is not just about external access, but about overcoming inner conditioning that limits what you believe is possible. Recognizing this mindset is the first step toward change.

Once you begin examining wealth through this lens, you notice patterns that repeat across time and culture. Those who create lasting fortunes rarely depend on a single source of income. Instead, they diversify their opportunities and structure their assets so that one success fuels another. The public often interprets this as luck or natural talent, but closer study shows it is deliberate strategy built on principles that have existed for centuries.

These principles involve leverage, timing, and positioning. Wealthy individuals place themselves where money naturally flows, often ahead of major shifts. They identify industries on the rise, secure ownership stakes before the crowd notices, and protect those gains through legal and financial frameworks. For outsiders, these moves seem invisible because they happen quietly and without fanfare. By the time the public recognizes an opportunity, insiders have already positioned themselves and are reaping the rewards.

The persistence of hidden wealth practices also comes from human nature itself. Societies create narratives that justify inequality, and these narratives often portray extraordinary wealth as unattainable for ordinary people. As long as most believe they are playing the same game, there is little pressure to question the rules. In reality, the game is layered: there are public rules, which everyone is taught, and private strategies, which circulate among those with access. Understanding this distinction is key to transforming your own approach to money and power.

Learning to See the Invisible

The first step in accessing hidden wealth strategies is awareness. Much of what keeps people from these opportunities is not deliberate exclusion but blindness. For example, early-stage investment rounds, specialized trusts, or off-market real estate deals are not secret in the literal sense; they simply exist in networks and conversations where most people do not participate. By broadening who you connect with and what you study, you start noticing pathways that once felt impossible.

This awareness also requires reframing how you think about money. Rather than seeing it as something to accumulate and protect, wealthy insiders view money as a tool to unlock more opportunities. They think in terms of systems rather than individual transactions. They consider not just how to earn but how to multiply, protect, and position wealth so it serves larger goals like influence, freedom, and legacy.

The Ethical Side of Hidden Wealth

It is natural to question whether using insider strategies is fair. History is filled with examples of corruption and exploitation, but this book does not advocate shortcuts that harm others or violate ethical boundaries. The true advantage lies in education and perspective. By learning the strategies of the elite, you are not taking from someone else's share; you are entering a bigger game where wealth creation expands what is possible for you and those you care about. Ethical wealth is sustainable wealth. It fosters trust, creates opportunities for others, and allows you to build influence without compromising your values.

When you begin to adopt these principles, the world starts to look different. Opportunities that once seemed random or reserved for others begin to appear within reach. You notice patterns in markets, relationships, and timing that others miss. More importantly, you realize that wealth is not solely about money. It is about freedom — freedom to choose how you spend your time, who you work with, and what legacy you leave behind.

The chapters ahead will guide you through these layers in detail. You will learn how to dismantle the psychological barriers that keep wealth hidden, uncover the frameworks that insiders use to multiply their resources, and begin applying these strategies to your own life. By the end, you will not just understand why wealth has always had a hidden side; you will be prepared to step into it yourself and use it ethically to create lasting impact.

How the Elite Play a Different Game (And Why It's Invisible to Most)

At first glance, wealth might appear to be the result of hard work, smart decisions, or simple luck. From the outside, it seems as if everyone is playing by the same rules, competing on the same field, and striving for the same outcomes. Yet when you study the habits and strategies of those at the top, a startling truth emerges: they are not just playing better; they are playing an entirely different game. This is not a figure of speech. The systems they navigate, the opportunities they see, and the metrics they prioritize are fundamentally unlike what most people have been taught to pursue.

The traditional game, the one most people are introduced to early in life, revolves around linear effort and incremental gain. It begins with the belief that financial success comes from steady employment, careful saving, and modest investing. Schools reinforce this narrative with lessons about budgeting and career planning, while mainstream financial advice echoes the same formula: minimize expenses, invest in retirement accounts, and wait decades for compound interest to do its work. For those playing this game, the reward is stability. The goal is a comfortable life, not extraordinary wealth.

The elite play by a separate set of rules. Their approach is built on leverage, access, and positioning rather than direct labor. They think in terms of multiplying opportunities rather than exchanging time for money. Instead of focusing on salaries, they prioritize ownership. Instead of waiting for permission or security, they seek ways to control the flow of resources and information. This is not about breaking the law or bending morality; it is about understanding that wealth creation happens in networks and layers invisible to those outside of them.

The Hidden Playing Field

One reason this game is invisible to most is that its pathways are rarely taught openly. Elite circles share information through private conversations, mentorships, and family exposure rather than through public education. A child raised in a household where parents invest in real estate or build companies grows up hearing about deal structures, equity stakes, and tax strategies in casual conversation. By adulthood, these concepts feel normal and attainable. Contrast that with the average household, where financial discussions often center on bills, wages, and saving for emergencies. The result is a quiet but profound divergence in mindset and opportunity.

Access compounds this divide. Many of the most lucrative opportunities are not listed publicly. They occur through personal introductions, private investment rounds, or closed professional circles. The sociologist Mark Granovetter demonstrated in 1973 that people often find their most valuable opportunities through "weak ties," connections beyond their immediate social group. The wealthy excel at cultivating these connections, giving them access to information and possibilities that others may never encounter. To outsiders, this looks like luck. In reality, it is strategy.

Different Metrics, Different Moves

Another reason the game feels invisible is that the elite measure success differently. While most people think in terms of income, the wealthy think in terms of equity, cash flow, and influence. A high salary means little compared to owning a percentage of a growing asset. Where the average person sees risk in starting a business or investing in emerging markets, insiders see an asymmetric opportunity — limited downside and massive upside if the move succeeds. This is why two individuals can work equally hard yet experience vastly different financial outcomes: they are measuring progress by different metrics and optimizing for different results.

Understanding this difference is not about envy; it is about awareness. Once you see the layers of the game, you can begin to shift your own strategies. The first step is to recognize where the rules you have been taught no longer serve you. The next is learning how to identify the hidden pathways the elite follow without blindly copying their actions. This requires clarity about your own goals and an honest assessment of the mindset shifts necessary to step into a different arena.

Even when people are introduced to these concepts, many struggle to integrate them because they conflict with ingrained habits and cultural conditioning. Shifting from earning wages to pursuing ownership, or from seeking stability to embracing calculated risk, requires more than new information. It requires unlearning patterns that have been reinforced for years. This is why, even with open access to books, courses, and financial tools, the gap between how the majority and the elite operate continues to widen. The challenge is not only about opportunity but also about perception and belief.

The elite approach risk differently because they view it through the lens of preparation and diversification rather than fear. Instead of asking, "What if this fails?" they ask, "How can I structure this so that failure costs little, but success changes everything?" This mindset enables them to pursue opportunities that others dismiss as too uncertain. It also allows them to act quickly when conditions shift. During financial downturns, for instance, while most people retreat and cut back, insiders often buy assets at discounts that later generate extraordinary returns. Their understanding of cycles, coupled with patience, turns chaos into opportunity.

Networks amplify these advantages. When someone in an elite circle learns about an emerging technology, a distressed property, or a regulatory change, that information spreads quietly among peers long before it becomes public knowledge. This does not mean insider trading or illegal activity; it reflects the natural flow of information in tightly connected groups. Those relationships form a kind of early warning system for opportunities and risks, giving them a significant edge over those who rely solely on mainstream media or public data.

A key difference is also found in how insiders use leverage. Most people think of leverage only as debt, often viewing it negatively. The wealthy understand that leverage extends far beyond borrowing money. They leverage other people's time, specialized knowledge, and systems to create results far greater than they could achieve alone. A single well-structured deal can produce returns that a lifetime of salaried work could never match. By thinking in systems rather than tasks, they free themselves from the limits of personal labor and unlock exponential growth.

Recognizing these patterns does not mean replicating every move of the elite. Many strategies require resources, access, or timing that the average person may not initially possess. What matters is learning the principles behind them and applying those principles at your own level. For example, you may not have capital for a large real estate portfolio, but you can still adopt the mindset of ownership by building skills or creating assets that generate recurring value. You can also expand your network intentionally, seeking out connections that expose you to perspectives and opportunities outside your current circle.

As you begin to internalize these shifts, the financial landscape starts to look different. The choices available to you widen. You see possibilities where before there were none. The invisible becomes visible, and the idea of playing a different game stops being abstract and starts feeling practical.

The Shift: From Outsider to Insider

There is a moment in every wealth journey when a person realizes that the rules they have been following are not the ones driving extraordinary results. This realization can feel disorienting. You work hard, follow advice you were told was sound, and yet see others advancing at a pace that seems impossible to replicate. The difference lies not only in what they know but in how they see. The shift from outsider to insider is less about acquiring money first and more about transforming perspective. Once you begin to see the game differently, you start playing differently, and eventually, you find yourself invited into circles you once thought were inaccessible.

Recognizing the Outsider Mindset

The outsider mindset is shaped by cultural conditioning. From a young age, most people are taught to prioritize security over growth, conformity over exploration, and predictability over boldness. This conditioning creates a financial script: go to school, get a good job, save consistently, and avoid risks that could disrupt stability. For many, this script feels safe, but it rarely leads to significant wealth. It prepares you for survival, not freedom.

An outsider tends to see opportunities only when they are obvious to everyone else. By the time an idea feels safe, the elite have already capitalized on it. Consider how ordinary investors often enter markets at their peak, lured by media hype, while insiders quietly bought in years earlier when prices were low and sentiment was uncertain. This delayed reaction is not due to lack of intelligence but to a difference in perspective and access. Outsiders follow public signals, while insiders operate based on private knowledge, patterns, and principles learned through experience and networks.

Another hallmark of the outsider mindset is linear thinking. Outsiders often believe that more effort equals more reward, leading to the assumption that wealth is purely a function of hard work. Insiders know this is not true. They understand that systems, leverage, and timing multiply results far beyond what personal effort can achieve. This realization marks the beginning of the shift — the recognition that working harder is not enough and that working differently is what matters.

The First Steps Toward Becoming an Insider

The transition begins internally. Before you can gain access to new opportunities, you must reshape how you approach money, power, and value creation. This involves examining your beliefs about wealth and questioning where those beliefs came from. Are they inherited from family, culture, or outdated advice? Do they reflect reality, or do they serve to keep you comfortable in the familiar?

A crucial part of this shift is reframing risk. Outsiders see risk as something to avoid. Insiders see risk as something to manage and, when possible, to use in their favor. They recognize that playing it safe often carries hidden risks, like inflation eroding savings or missed chances that will never come again. By learning how to analyze and mitigate risk, you can start approaching opportunities with a clearer, calmer mindset rather than reacting from fear.

This process also involves cultivating new skills and perspectives. You do not need immediate wealth to think like an insider. You need curiosity, humility, and a willingness to step outside familiar environments. Expanding your network, learning from those ahead of you, and exposing yourself to new industries or markets begins to shift how you perceive opportunities. Over time, this exposure compounds, and you begin to notice options that others overlook.

The most important part of this transition is understanding that the door is not permanently closed. Becoming an insider is not about being born into privilege but about developing the mindset and behaviors that attract insider opportunities.

As you progress along this path, the world around you begins to reveal layers that were always present but previously invisible. You start recognizing patterns in conversations, in market trends, and in the ways people of influence move. This awareness creates a subtle but powerful shift: you no longer feel like an outsider trying to gain entry, but rather someone capable of decoding the signals and navigating them with intention.

The change is not instantaneous. It unfolds as you build trust, competence, and a reputation for reliability. Insiders are not impressed by words or appearances; they watch actions, consistency, and the value you bring to the table. One of the fastest ways to bridge the gap is to focus on contribution.

Ask what you can offer to networks or individuals you aspire to learn from, rather than what they can give you. This mindset of service creates reciprocity and opens doors that would remain closed to someone seeking only personal gain.

Financially, the transition requires shifting from short-term rewards to long-term positioning. Outsiders often prioritize immediate comfort, spending gains as soon as they arrive or chasing the next visible milestone. Insiders, on the other hand, are willing to delay gratification to build enduring assets. They think in decades rather than months. This patience, coupled with a deep understanding of compounding, allows them to make moves that seem modest at first but grow exponentially over time.

The process also involves becoming fluent in the language of insiders. This does not mean using jargon to impress, but rather understanding key concepts like equity, liquidity, and leverage well enough to evaluate opportunities intelligently. Once you grasp these fundamentals, you are no longer at the mercy of vague promises or hype. You can discern which opportunities align with your goals and which are distractions. Knowledge in this context is both protection and power.

Over time, as you internalize these shifts, something else happens: you begin creating opportunities rather than waiting for them. Instead of asking to join someone else's table, you start building your own. This is the ultimate sign that you have crossed the threshold. The outsider waits for permission. The insider creates access — not just for themselves, but eventually for others who are ready to rise.

Making this leap does not erase all challenges. It requires continuous learning, humility, and the ability to navigate complexity. Yet once you experience life on the other side of that threshold, it is impossible to go back to the old way of thinking. You recognize that the biggest transformation was never only about money. It was about expanding what you believe is possible and stepping into a role where you shape your future rather than simply reacting to it.

This shift is the foundation for everything that follows in this book. As we move deeper into the strategies and principles that govern hidden wealth, keep this idea in mind: the goal is not to imitate the elite, but to learn the timeless rules they follow and apply them in a way that aligns with your own values. That is how you build not only wealth, but also the freedom and legacy that wealth is meant to serve.

Part I. Foundations of Hidden Wealth

Every structure, no matter how tall or complex, rests on foundations. Wealth is no different. The fortunes we see in the world — the empires, the legacies, the families who quietly control industries — are not built on luck or isolated windfalls. They rest on principles that are rarely discussed openly yet shape how money flows, grows, and endures. Before we explore advanced strategies, it is essential to uncover these foundations and understand why they remain hidden from most people.

This part of the book is about pulling back that curtain. It will reveal why traditional financial advice, while useful for stability, often keeps people from playing the real wealth game. It will show you how the systems that govern money have existed for centuries, evolving with technology and global markets yet still rooted in timeless dynamics. Most importantly, it will begin reshaping how you think about value, power, and the kind of freedom wealth can create.

The shift you are about to make is not about greed or chasing status. It is about reclaiming agency over your financial life. Many people unknowingly accept a role as spectators, believing that extraordinary wealth is reserved for those born into privilege or those who get lucky. This belief blinds them to opportunities available in plain sight and discourages them from seeking the knowledge that could change everything. By understanding the foundations of hidden wealth, you stop waiting for permission and start learning how to participate intentionally.

What follows will challenge assumptions. You will see why the elite measure success differently, why they prioritize ownership over income, and why their strategies appear invisible to outsiders. You will also discover that these approaches are not inherently unreachable. While access may look exclusive, the principles themselves can be learned and adapted at any level, provided you are willing to think differently and act deliberately.

By the time you complete this part, you will have a new lens for evaluating every financial decision you make. You will understand how the game is truly played and begin laying the groundwork for strategies that build not only wealth but the freedom and influence that come with it. This is where the journey shifts from curiosity to clarity — and from clarity to action.

Chapter 1: The Hidden Architecture of Money

Unseen Systems That Govern Wealth

Most people grow up believing wealth is a direct outcome of visible actions: working harder, saving diligently, and climbing the professional ladder. While these behaviors can create stability, they rarely lead to extraordinary wealth. The truth is that the largest fortunes are built and protected through systems that operate quietly in the background. These systems are not secret in the sense of being hidden by law; they are hidden in plain sight, overlooked by those who have never been taught to recognize them.

Understanding these systems is the first step toward leveling the playing field. Without this awareness, even the most motivated person will find themselves operating within limits they cannot see. They might believe they are making smart financial decisions while unknowingly playing a game designed to cap their potential. By uncovering these mechanisms, you shift from being a participant in someone else's system to building one of your own.

The Framework of Financial Infrastructure

At the core of modern wealth creation are financial infrastructures that determine how money flows and grows. Corporations, trusts, holding companies, and investment vehicles are tools that the wealthy use to multiply their resources. They provide advantages in taxation, liability protection, and scale that ordinary individuals rarely access. For example, while most people earn wages subject to the highest tax brackets, business owners and investors structure income in ways that legally minimize taxation and maximize reinvestment. This is not about exploiting loopholes; it is about understanding the rules of the system and using them intelligently. Thomas Piketty's research in *Capital in the Twenty-First Century* (2014) demonstrated how capital, rather than labor, drives the majority of wealth accumulation. His findings revealed that when returns on capital outpace economic growth, those who own assets naturally become wealthier over time, while wage earners struggle to keep up. This single insight explains why the rich focus on acquiring and holding appreciating assets rather than trading time for money. The system rewards ownership, not effort alone.

How Networks Reinforce the System

Another invisible mechanism is the role of networks in amplifying wealth. Opportunities rarely appear in public view. They circulate within trusted circles long before the wider market becomes aware of them. These networks are not just social; they are structural. Boards of directors, private equity groups, and family offices share information and coordinate moves that outsiders never hear about.

For someone on the outside, it may appear as though the wealthy simply stumble upon deals or investments at the right moment. In reality, these opportunities flow predictably through relationship pipelines. Access to information, introductions to decision-makers, and early entry into rising markets are all advantages built on trust and reputation. While this may seem unfair, it highlights a principle you can apply even at smaller scales: building relationships opens doors that pure hard work cannot.

Psychological Systems Behind Wealth

Beyond structures and networks, there is a psychological system that governs how the elite make decisions. They view money as a tool, not as an end in itself. This mental framing changes how they respond to risk, how they value time, and how they evaluate opportunities. Most people hesitate to act on uncertain possibilities, focusing instead on preserving what they have. Insiders see uncertainty differently; they design strategies that minimize downside while maximizing upside. Over time, this approach allows them to capitalize on opportunities others are too cautious to pursue. Understanding these mental models is just as important as understanding legal or financial structures. Without adopting the mindset that wealth requires, you may know the mechanics but still hesitate to apply them. The hidden system is not only external; it is internal, shaping decisions every day. This awareness also brings clarity about why many people feel stuck despite working hard. Traditional advice focuses on budgeting, avoiding debt, and steadily contributing to retirement accounts. While these practices promote financial safety, they rarely generate transformative outcomes. Safety nets are important, but they are not engines of wealth. The systems that truly build fortunes involve positioning yourself to benefit from compounding growth, scalable opportunities, and access to tools that amplify results over time.

Once you see this distinction, it becomes clear why so few people break out of the cycle of exchanging time for money. The average person experiences money linearly: one hour of work equals one unit of pay. Wealthy individuals experience money exponentially: one smart decision or structure can generate returns for years without additional labor. For example, establishing a business entity or investment trust might take effort up front but can provide ongoing tax advantages, asset protection, and income far beyond what hourly work can deliver.

The legal frameworks that enable this are openly documented yet poorly understood by most. Tax codes, corporate law, and investment regulations appear complicated, which discourages outsiders from exploring them. Insiders either learn these rules directly or surround themselves with experts who do. This is why elite families and entrepreneurs often rely on specialized advisors to create strategies tailored to their goals. They understand that paying for expertise is not an expense but an investment that multiplies over time.

Networks operate in a similar way. As you move closer to circles where financial opportunities circulate, you realize that information is rarely broadcast widely. Deals are discussed quietly, introductions are made selectively, and trust is built gradually. Those who consistently provide value to their networks are invited into more rooms, hear about more opportunities, and gain access to insights before they reach the public. This is not limited to billionaires or CEOs; it applies on smaller scales as well. Even within local communities, being part of the right conversations can reveal paths that others simply never encounter.

Psychology plays the most personal role in navigating these systems. It is one thing to understand structures and access; it is another to trust yourself to act when an opportunity appears. Fear of loss, skepticism, and self-doubt often hold people back more than lack of knowledge. Studies in behavioral economics, such as those by Richard Thaler in 2015, show how mental shortcuts and biases lead individuals to make decisions that undermine long-term growth. Recognizing these patterns allows you to counteract them and make choices aligned with your larger goals rather than immediate comfort. Applying these insights begins with observation. Look at where your financial habits reflect the traditional script and where you might begin to integrate insider principles. Consider shifting your focus from immediate income to building or acquiring assets. Explore how to form relationships that expand your perspective and connect you with knowledge you would not find on your own. Most importantly, commit to reframing how you perceive risk and opportunity, understanding that the greatest rewards often come from decisions that feel uncomfortable at first.

Why Traditional Advice Keeps You Average

Conventional financial wisdom promises security. Work hard, save consistently, avoid debt, and invest in safe, long-term vehicles like retirement accounts. At first glance, this guidance seems sensible. It protects you from major pitfalls and creates stability in uncertain times. Yet if you look at the outcomes of those who follow it closely, one thing becomes clear: very few become truly wealthy. They might retire comfortably, but they rarely achieve the level of financial freedom that allows them to design their life on their own terms.

This is not because the advice is malicious or entirely wrong. It is because it is incomplete. Traditional financial advice is designed for the masses. It simplifies complex realities into digestible rules so that most people can avoid financial disaster. While these rules keep you safe, they also keep you average. They prevent you from seeing opportunities that require more nuanced thinking and from taking actions that might feel uncomfortable but lead to transformative results.

The One-Size-Fits-All Problem

Most mainstream advice is built on a single narrative: the linear path of education, employment, saving, and retirement. It assumes that everyone wants the same outcomes and should follow the same steps to get there. This model worked reasonably well in past decades when pensions were common, wages kept pace with living costs, and investing opportunities were limited. Today, the landscape is different. Inflation erodes savings faster, markets move in unpredictable cycles, and new opportunities arise outside the narrow lanes of retirement accounts and traditional employment.

Yet financial education for the general public has barely changed. Schools still teach budgeting but rarely explore ownership, equity, or leverage. Media personalities caution against risk but rarely explain how to manage it intelligently. The result is a generation of people who know how to avoid mistakes but do not know how to build extraordinary outcomes. They play defense without ever learning offense.

The Illusion of Safety

Traditional advice often glorifies safety without acknowledging its hidden costs. Keeping money in savings accounts or low-yield investments feels secure, but over time inflation silently diminishes its value. Avoiding all debt may prevent financial strain in the short term, yet it also prevents you from using leverage strategically to acquire appreciating assets or build businesses. The pursuit of safety becomes its own form of risk: the risk of stagnation. This mindset can be traced back to cultural conditioning. For decades, the dominant narrative equated risk with danger and equated security with virtue. People were praised for living within their means and warned against ambitions that seemed "too big." These lessons were meant to protect families from ruin but inadvertently created ceilings that kept them from wealth. The wealthy, in contrast, do not avoid risk; they learn to manage and direct it. They see safety not as the absence of risk but as the ability to withstand and recover from it.

The Time-for-Money Trap

Another flaw in traditional advice is its focus on trading time for money. The idea that working more hours or finding a higher-paying job will solve financial challenges seems logical but has limits. Time is finite, and income tied to personal labor rarely scales. The wealthy escape this trap by shifting from earning income to owning assets and systems that generate income independently. They prioritize building equity rather than simply increasing wages.

For those raised on conventional guidance, this shift can feel radical. It challenges the belief that hard work alone leads to success. While effort is important, the key is where that effort is applied. Working harder at the wrong game only entrenches average results. Understanding this distinction is essential for breaking out of the cycle.

This widespread adherence to traditional advice persists in part because it feels comfortable and socially validated. Friends, family, and even financial media often reinforce the same messages: avoid risk, save what you can, and be content with gradual progress. Challenging these beliefs can feel isolating, as though stepping outside accepted norms invites judgment or criticism. Yet the very path that feels safe is often the one that guarantees mediocrity, because it prevents people from exploring the strategies that truly build freedom and lasting wealth.

Another reason traditional advice remains dominant is that it benefits existing systems. Employers prefer employees who focus on stable careers rather than ownership, because it ensures a consistent labor force. Financial institutions profit from encouraging widespread participation in products like mutual funds and retirement accounts, which generate fees over decades. There is nothing inherently wrong with these products, but they are rarely the tools that create generational wealth. They maintain the status quo, providing incremental gains rather than transformative ones.

Breaking away from these patterns requires questioning the assumptions behind them. For example, the advice to "save for retirement" implies a future where you no longer generate income and rely solely on what you accumulated. Insiders approach this differently. They focus on building assets that produce income indefinitely, so retirement becomes optional rather than a point of necessity. Their goal is financial independence long before conventional retirement age, achieved not through decades of slow saving but through ownership and strategic growth.

A major shift occurs when you stop asking only how to cut expenses and start asking how to expand opportunities. Traditional advice tends to emphasize frugality, but there is a ceiling to how much you can save. There is no ceiling to how much value you can create, how many assets you can acquire, or how effectively you can position yourself in emerging markets. This does not mean reckless spending; it means redirecting energy from pure cost-cutting to building income streams that make those costs negligible.

Psychology plays a central role here. Traditional advice fosters a defensive mindset — one that views wealth as fragile and easily lost. Insiders cultivate an expansive mindset. They understand that setbacks are temporary and that the greatest risk is staying still. By reframing failure as feedback and seeing money as a tool rather than a scarce resource, they make decisions others shy away from. This psychological shift is what allows them to enter spaces where opportunities compound instead of diminish.

Recognizing these limitations does not mean rejecting every element of conventional wisdom. Disciplined saving, avoiding destructive debt, and living below your means can provide stability, especially in the early stages of building wealth. The danger lies in mistaking these practices for the end goal rather than the starting point. They are the foundation, not the framework. Once stability is secured, growth demands a different approach — one that prioritizes ownership, leverage, and strategic positioning.

By identifying where traditional advice falls short, you open the door to a new set of possibilities. You can begin blending the best of both worlds: using foundational habits to stay grounded while adopting insider strategies to accelerate growth. This combination creates resilience and momentum, preparing you to move beyond survival and into a phase where wealth becomes a tool for freedom and impact rather than simply a means to cover expenses.

Shifting from Linear to Exponential Thinking

The way you think about growth shapes every decision you make with money, time, and energy. Most people operate with a linear mindset, believing that progress happens in straight, predictable lines. Work a certain number of hours, receive a certain paycheck. Save a certain percentage each month, watch your bank account grow by small increments. This model feels intuitive because it matches early experiences — study harder, get better grades; work longer, earn more income. Yet when it comes to wealth, linear thinking traps you at the level of predictable results.

Exponential thinking operates differently. It recognizes that certain actions, when aligned with the right systems, create growth that accelerates over time. Instead of adding one unit at a time, exponential moves multiply results in ways that seem almost invisible at first and overwhelming later. Compounding interest is the most obvious example: small, consistent investments appear modest in the early years but balloon dramatically in later stages. However, compounding applies to far more than money. Knowledge, networks, and reputation also compound, creating opportunities that expand beyond what linear effort alone can achieve.

The Limits of Linear Thinking

Linear thinking encourages you to measure success by immediate outputs. It rewards visible effort: the hours you work, the tasks you complete, the short-term milestones you achieve. While this mindset is not inherently wrong, it becomes limiting when applied to wealth creation. There are only so many hours you can work, only so many promotions you can earn, only so many expenses you can cut. Even with discipline and dedication, linear strategies reach a ceiling.

This ceiling explains why so many high earners remain financially constrained. They have mastered the linear game, trading time for money at increasingly higher rates, yet they lack assets or systems that grow without their constant input. When income stops, growth stops. The elite avoid this trap by focusing on strategies that separate growth from direct labor. They prioritize building mechanisms that generate value on their own, whether through investments, intellectual property, or scalable businesses.

Understanding Exponential Leverage

Exponential thinking is not about working harder but about identifying levers that amplify results. These levers include capital, technology, networks, and knowledge. When combined, they create opportunities where small actions yield disproportionate returns. For example, creating a digital product requires effort once but can be sold repeatedly with minimal additional cost. Acquiring equity in a business can generate dividends for years without further labor.

The shift begins by reframing how you evaluate opportunities. Instead of asking, "How much can I earn for this amount of work?" ask, "How can this decision create ongoing growth beyond the initial effort?" This perspective encourages you to seek scalable options rather than purely transactional ones. It also fosters patience, as exponential gains often take time to reveal themselves. The early stages of building an asset can feel slow, but over time the results accelerate in ways that surprise those accustomed to linear progress.

Why Most People Resist This Shift

Despite its advantages, exponential thinking is uncomfortable at first. It challenges deeply ingrained beliefs about work, reward, and security. Many people are conditioned to trust immediate returns and fear delayed gratification. They prefer the certainty of a paycheck over the uncertainty of an investment, even when the potential upside is far greater. Behavioral studies, including those by Walter Mischel in 1972, highlight how the ability to delay gratification strongly correlates with long-term success. Yet most individuals struggle with this discipline, preferring small, quick wins over larger future gains.

Shifting mindset requires more than understanding the math behind compounding; it requires training yourself to tolerate uncertainty and to act on opportunities that may not pay off right away. This mental adjustment is a defining trait of insiders. They accept that building wealth often involves planting seeds that take years to mature, confident that the eventual harvest will justify the wait.

Applying exponential thinking begins with reevaluating where you direct your effort. If your current path relies entirely on your time and energy to produce results, it is by definition limited. Building or acquiring assets that can grow and operate without your constant involvement shifts you into a different trajectory. This might mean starting a small business that can scale beyond you, investing in rental properties that generate consistent cash flow, or developing intellectual property like a book, course, or software that can be distributed indefinitely once created. Each of these approaches turns a single action into a source of ongoing growth.

The principle extends to relationships and networks. A single connection can lead to opportunities far greater than any effort you could achieve alone. By cultivating authentic relationships, sharing value, and positioning yourself in circles aligned with growth, you create ripple effects that unfold over years. The right introduction or partnership can open doors to investments, collaborations, or insights unavailable through traditional channels. Insiders understand this and spend significant energy nurturing relationships because they know how disproportionate the returns can be.

Technology is another lever that transforms linear effort into exponential outcomes. Tools that automate, amplify, or distribute work allow individuals to accomplish in months what once required years. A message shared online can reach thousands or even millions, while traditional efforts might have influenced only a handful. Those who learn to harness technology not only expand their reach but also remove themselves from the constant grind of direct labor. They design systems where output continues even when they step away.

The mental shift required to embrace this approach involves becoming comfortable with delayed visibility. Exponential growth often feels invisible in the early stages because results appear small and incremental. It is only after a tipping point that progress accelerates and becomes obvious to others. This is why patience and conviction are essential. Outsiders may abandon promising strategies too early because they misinterpret the slow start as failure, while insiders remain committed, understanding how compounding works.

Practical application of this mindset involves asking better questions. Instead of focusing solely on how to earn more in the next month, consider how each decision affects your life over the next five or ten years. Does this choice create assets or merely income? Does it build skills or connections that multiply opportunities in the future? Does it position you closer to ownership rather than dependency? By consistently framing decisions this way, you train yourself to prioritize moves that generate lasting impact rather than temporary relief.

This way of thinking also demands a willingness to take calculated risks. While exponential opportunities offer high potential rewards, they often involve ambiguity and longer timelines. The key is to structure decisions so that losses are manageable while gains are significant. This asymmetric approach — minimizing downside while maximizing upside — allows you to participate in opportunities that can transform your financial trajectory without jeopardizing stability.

Ultimately, shifting from linear to exponential thinking is not about abandoning security or taking reckless bets. It is about evolving from a mindset of addition to one of multiplication, from immediate gratification to long-term creation. By embracing this shift, you begin to see possibilities that others overlook and position yourself for growth that accelerates rather than stagnates. This is the foundation upon which the strategies of the elite are built, and adopting it is the first step toward entering that game yourself.

Chapter 2: Mindset of the Wealth Insider

Scarcity vs. Abundance Psychology

The way you perceive the world directly shapes the decisions you make with money and opportunities. For many, the default lens is scarcity: the belief that resources are limited, that success is a zero-sum game, and that someone else's gain must come at their expense. This mindset is deeply rooted in survival instincts and reinforced by cultural narratives that glorify caution and competition. While scarcity thinking can protect you in moments of crisis, it also silently restricts growth. It narrows your field of vision, making you focus on what you lack rather than what you can create. In contrast, abundance psychology views resources, opportunities, and wealth as expansive rather than fixed. It does not deny challenges or constraints but operates from the understanding that new value can always be generated. People who adopt this mindset look for ways to expand the pie instead of fighting for the smallest slice. They collaborate more freely, take calculated risks more confidently, and recognize possibilities that others dismiss as unrealistic. This perspective does not emerge from naivety; it comes from understanding how systems of wealth actually work and how value multiplies when cultivated deliberately.

The Cost of Scarcity Thinking

Scarcity thinking shapes financial behavior in subtle but powerful ways. It leads to hoarding rather than investing, hesitating rather than acting, and competing rather than collaborating. Someone operating in scarcity might see every opportunity as a potential threat. They avoid sharing ideas for fear of being copied, miss out on partnerships because they cannot trust others, and resist growth because it feels unsafe. Over time, this mindset creates a self-fulfilling cycle: fear of lack leads to inaction, which reinforces the very limitations they hoped to escape.

This perspective also influences how people interpret success. When you view life as a finite game, someone else's achievement feels like evidence of your own inadequacy. Instead of seeing role models as proof that something is possible, scarcity thinking frames them as competitors who are "taking" what could have been yours. This creates envy rather than inspiration, and it blinds you to lessons that could accelerate your own journey.

The effects extend beyond finances. Scarcity thinking affects time, relationships, and even creativity. If you constantly feel there is "never enough," you may undervalue rest, neglect long-term planning, or resist delegating tasks to others. This hyper-focus on conserving what you have often prevents you from building something greater.

The Power of Abundance Psychology

Abundance psychology begins with a shift in focus from limitation to possibility. It does not ignore the realities of constraint but asks, "How can I create more?" rather than "How can I hold on to what little I have?" This approach invites resourcefulness. Instead of being paralyzed by what is missing, you begin to see overlooked assets — skills, networks, and opportunities that can be combined in new ways.

Those who embrace abundance are more willing to share knowledge and collaborate, recognizing that mutual benefit often leads to greater outcomes than solitary efforts. This is evident in high-level networks where introductions, advice, and resources circulate freely among members. The trust built within these circles creates a multiplier effect. One act of generosity often leads to opportunities returning many times over, though not always from the same source.

This mindset also fosters resilience. When setbacks occur, scarcity thinkers interpret them as confirmation of failure or proof that success is impossible. Abundance thinkers, however, view setbacks as part of the process. They understand that growth is cyclical and that lessons from challenges often lead to stronger foundations for future success. This does not mean ignoring risk or living recklessly; it means recognizing that fear cannot be the primary driver of decisions.

Understanding the distinction between these two mindsets is critical because it determines how you respond to opportunities and challenges alike.

Making the transition to abundance thinking requires deliberate effort because scarcity patterns are often deeply ingrained. The first step is awareness. You cannot shift what you cannot see. Begin by observing your internal dialogue when faced with opportunities or challenges. Do you instinctively think in terms of what could go wrong, or do you consider what might be possible? This awareness allows you to interrupt automatic reactions and consciously choose a different perspective.

Exposure to new environments accelerates this shift. Surrounding yourself with people who think expansively helps rewire your own beliefs about what is possible. In rooms where others are discussing investments, building businesses, or creating collaborations, abundance becomes the norm rather than the exception. This does not mean blindly adopting someone else's mindset, but rather absorbing proof that opportunities are more plentiful than you may have believed. Seeing real examples of people creating value in unconventional ways challenges the assumption that resources are limited.

A critical component of abundance psychology is learning to trust your ability to create and adapt. Scarcity thinking clings to what is known because it fears the unknown. Abundance thinking understands that skills, creativity, and resilience can generate new solutions even when circumstances change. This trust grows through action. Each time you take a calculated step toward growth — investing in learning, building relationships, or launching a new idea — you gather evidence that you can navigate uncertainty and recover from setbacks. Over time, this builds confidence to pursue opportunities others avoid.

Another practical way to cultivate abundance is to focus on value creation rather than accumulation. When you shift from "How can I get more?" to "How can I create more value?" you open doors to wealth in forms beyond money. Providing value to others leads to reciprocity, stronger networks, and opportunities that compound over time. This orientation also makes wealth-building more sustainable, as it is grounded in service rather than extraction.

It is equally important to redefine what "enough" means. Abundance does not imply constant striving or endless accumulation. It is about knowing you have the capacity to create and access what you need when you need it. This perspective quiets the anxiety that drives unhealthy comparison and impulsive decision-making. From this grounded place, you can pursue growth without fear of loss dictating every move.

Integrating abundance thinking does not happen overnight. It requires consistent practice, reflection, and recalibration, especially when challenges arise. Old patterns will resurface, particularly during financial stress or uncertainty. The difference is that now you have tools to recognize them and choose differently. Each choice to act from possibility rather than fear strengthens the habit, until it becomes your default way of operating.

By cultivating this shift, you position yourself to see opportunities invisible to most. You begin to recognize that wealth is not a fixed resource but something that expands as you learn, connect, and create. This perspective lays the psychological groundwork for everything that follows in your journey toward hidden wealth. Without it, even the best strategies remain underutilized. With it, every action you take is amplified, because you are no longer operating from limitation but from the understanding that growth is available and within reach.

The Power of Cognitive Reframing

The way you interpret events often matters more than the events themselves. Two people can experience the same setback — a failed investment, a job loss, a missed opportunity — and walk away with completely different outcomes. One views it as evidence they are unlucky or unworthy and withdraws from taking future risks. The other sees it as feedback, adjusts their strategy, and uses the lesson to create greater success later. This difference is not about intelligence or resources; it is about framing. Cognitive reframing is the practice of deliberately changing the meaning you assign to experiences so that they empower rather than limit you.

In the context of wealth building, reframing is indispensable. The journey to financial freedom involves uncertainty, obstacles, and inevitable setbacks. Without reframing, these challenges easily become excuses to quit. With reframing, they become catalysts for growth. This is why insiders often seem unusually resilient. They are not immune to difficulties; they have trained themselves to interpret difficulties as part of the process rather than proof that the process does not work.

Understanding Cognitive Frames

A cognitive frame is essentially the lens through which you view a situation. It shapes your emotional response, the options you consider, and the actions you take. Scarcity, fear, or fixed-mindset frames lead to avoidance and inaction, while growth-oriented frames lead to curiosity and problem solving. The same event — for example, losing money in an investment — can be framed as catastrophic failure or as tuition paid for a valuable lesson. The frame you choose directly influences what happens next.

Research in psychology supports this. Carol Dweck's work on mindset in 2006 demonstrated that people who adopt a growth frame interpret challenges as opportunities to learn, while those with a fixed frame see them as threats to their identity. Similarly, studies on cognitive behavioral therapy show that reframing negative thoughts reduces stress and improves decision-making. In wealth building, where uncertainty and emotional volatility are constant, the ability to reframe quickly can mean the difference between staying the course and abandoning it prematurely.

Why Reframing Matters in Wealth Creation

Traditional financial advice often ignores the emotional side of money, focusing instead on numbers and tactics. Yet emotions drive behavior. Fear of loss leads to selling assets at the worst possible time. Overconfidence leads to reckless decisions during booms. Shame about past mistakes prevents people from seeking advice or trying again. Reframing interrupts these cycles by shifting focus from the emotional sting of the event to the information it offers.

For example, imagine launching a side business that does not succeed. A scarcity frame might say, "I wasted time and money. I should not try again." An abundance-oriented reframe might say, "I learned what does not work, and I now have insights to make the next attempt better." Both are interpretations of the same reality, yet one keeps you stuck while the other moves you forward.

This skill becomes even more valuable as stakes grow. Larger opportunities involve larger risks, and setbacks can feel heavier. Without reframing, even successful individuals can become paralyzed by fear of repeating mistakes. Insiders guard against this by normalizing failure as part of iteration. They treat every outcome — win or loss — as data for refining future decisions rather than as a verdict on their worth or potential.

Training the Reframe

Cognitive reframing is not about blind optimism or pretending problems do not exist. It is about accurate perspective. The practice begins with noticing your initial interpretation of an event and asking whether it is the only possible explanation. From there, you deliberately choose a frame that highlights possibilities, lessons, or next steps instead of limitations. This does not eliminate discomfort but shifts the energy toward constructive action.

One of the simplest ways to begin reframing is to question the meaning you automatically assign to setbacks. Instead of asking, "Why is this happening to me?" shift to "What can I learn from this?" or "How does this prepare me for what is next?" These questions turn passive suffering into active problem solving. They pull you out of the emotional fog and into a position of agency, where your choices can influence the outcome rather than being dictated by it.

This approach also helps manage the emotional volatility that wealth building inevitably triggers. Markets rise and fall. Businesses succeed and fail. Relationships evolve as financial circumstances change. A person locked into a rigid frame sees these shifts as destabilizing and threatening. Someone skilled in reframing sees them as natural cycles to be navigated rather than catastrophes to be avoided. This mental flexibility prevents reactive decisions that often do more damage than the events themselves.

Practical application involves pausing long enough to recognize when your frame is distorting your perception. If you notice intense emotional reactions — fear, anger, shame — it is often a signal that your interpretation needs adjustment. Naming the feeling, identifying the thought behind it, and deliberately considering alternative perspectives can interrupt destructive cycles. Over time, this becomes instinctive. You begin to see patterns and respond with curiosity rather than panic.

Reframing is also essential for interpreting opportunities. Many people overlook possibilities because they appear risky or unconventional at first glance. By shifting the frame from "This is too uncertain" to "What would make this safe enough to try?" you open pathways that others dismiss prematurely. This does not mean ignoring real risks; it means approaching them creatively. Often, the difference between fear and action lies in reframing the challenge into a solvable problem rather than an insurmountable obstacle.

There is also a deeper benefit to reframing that extends beyond immediate decisions. Over time, it transforms identity. When you repeatedly choose empowering frames, you stop seeing yourself as a passive participant in life and begin seeing yourself as a builder, a learner, and an agent of change. This identity shift alters how you pursue goals, interact with others, and envision your future. You become less reactive to circumstances and more intentional in shaping them.

Developing this habit requires consistent practice. Journaling about challenging events and deliberately rewriting their meaning is one effective method. Another is surrounding yourself with people who naturally reframe in constructive ways. Their language, optimism, and resilience can help normalize this perspective until it becomes part of your own thinking. Each small act of reframing compounds, building emotional resilience that supports bigger risks and bolder visions.

Ultimately, cognitive reframing equips you to face the unpredictable journey of building wealth with clarity and calm. It allows you to extract lessons from every experience, maintain focus during setbacks, and sustain the optimism needed for long-term growth. When paired with strategic action, this skill becomes one of the most powerful advantages you can develop — a quiet discipline that separates those who abandon their goals at the first sign of difficulty from those who adapt, persist, and eventually succeed.

Wealth Identity: Becoming Who You Must Be to Build It

Wealth is not only about numbers on a balance sheet. It begins with identity — who you believe yourself to be, what you believe you deserve, and how you act based on those beliefs. Two people can receive the same opportunity, but their results will differ dramatically if one sees themselves as someone capable of building and managing wealth while the other secretly believes they are unworthy of it or destined to lose it. The internal blueprint always dictates the external outcome.

This is why many people who win the lottery or come into sudden financial windfalls lose their money within a few years. They receive wealth without becoming the type of person who can sustain it. Their habits, mindset, and sense of self are still rooted in scarcity or survival. Without an internal shift, the external gain cannot last. The reverse is also true: people who develop a wealth identity often find that money begins to flow more easily, not because life becomes magically simpler, but because their decisions, habits, and opportunities align with their new sense of self.

Understanding Wealth Identity

Your identity is the story you tell yourself about who you are and what is possible for you. It influences every decision, often unconsciously. If you see yourself as someone who struggles financially, you will make choices that confirm that story — hesitating on opportunities, undervaluing your skills, or avoiding financial conversations altogether. If you see yourself as someone who builds and sustains wealth, you begin to act in ways that reinforce that belief — seeking information, taking calculated risks, and managing resources strategically.

Wealth identity is not about pretending to be rich or adopting superficial signals of success. It is about embodying the qualities that allow wealth to grow naturally: responsibility, vision, patience, and the willingness to learn and adapt. These qualities are available to anyone, regardless of starting point. The challenge lies in unlearning limiting beliefs and consciously constructing a new internal framework that supports the life you want to create.

The Role of Belief in Financial Growth

Beliefs shape behavior, and behavior shapes results. If deep down you believe that money is scarce, that wealthy people are greedy, or that success is always fleeting, you will subconsciously sabotage your own efforts. This self-sabotage might look like procrastinating on opportunities, abandoning strategies at the first sign of difficulty, or overspending as soon as income increases.

Research on self-concept supports this connection. Psychologist Albert Bandura's work on self-efficacy demonstrated that people's beliefs about their capabilities strongly predict their actual performance. In other words, believing you are capable of achieving wealth makes you more likely to take the actions required to achieve it. This does not mean belief alone creates results — action is essential — but belief fuels the consistency and resilience needed for those actions to compound over time.

Building a New Internal Blueprint

Shaping wealth identity begins with awareness of the old one. Reflect on the financial messages you absorbed growing up: what did your family teach you about money? Was it a source of stress, secrecy, or conflict? Did you hear phrases like "We can't afford that" or "Money doesn't grow on trees"? These statements often plant beliefs that persist into adulthood, even when circumstances change.

To shift into a new identity, you must challenge these inherited narratives. Begin by asking whether they are universally true or simply reflections of someone else's experience. Replacing them with new beliefs is not about blind optimism but about choosing perspectives that empower rather than limit you. For example, "Money is hard to make" can become "Money flows to value, and I can create value." This subtle shift opens possibilities your old story might have closed off.

The next step is to align daily actions with the identity you want to adopt. If you want to see yourself as someone who manages wealth well, start by managing whatever resources you currently have with intention. If you want to see yourself as an investor, begin learning about investment vehicles and practicing with small amounts. The identity becomes real through repetition and evidence — each aligned action reinforces the belief, until it becomes part of how you naturally operate.

Sustaining this shift requires consistent reinforcement. The mind tends to default to familiar patterns, especially under stress. When financial challenges arise, old beliefs can resurface, whispering that you are not capable or that success is temporary. This is where deliberate practices such as reflection, journaling, and intentional self-talk become crucial. By revisiting your progress, acknowledging how far you have come, and reminding yourself of the principles you now live by, you prevent setbacks from pulling you back into outdated narratives.

Equally important is surrounding yourself with environments that reflect your new identity. Identity is reinforced not only internally but externally. The conversations you have, the people you spend time with, and the content you consume either support or undermine your growth. Immersing yourself in communities that normalize ambition and responsible wealth creation accelerates your evolution. Being around people who discuss investments, strategy, and impact reframes what you consider normal and possible. Over time, this social proof quiets doubts and strengthens the belief that wealth building is simply part of who you are.

Your habits also become a mirror of your identity. Consistent small actions — tracking expenses, reviewing investments, setting goals — reinforce the image of someone who is intentional with money. Over time, these habits create compounding results, both financially and psychologically. Each aligned action sends a subtle message to your subconscious: "This is who I am now." This is why identity work is more sustainable than relying solely on motivation. Motivation can fade, but identity-driven habits become automatic.

Another aspect of wealth identity is redefining your relationship with responsibility. As your resources grow, so does the influence you hold over others, whether that is family, employees, or your broader community. Viewing wealth through this lens of stewardship rather than possession transforms how you manage it. It shifts focus from short-term gratification to long-term impact. Many of the world's most enduring fortunes are built not just on accumulation but on a sense of purpose that extends beyond personal gain.

Adopting this perspective also protects against the fear of loss. When your sense of identity is rooted in your ability to create and adapt rather than in the amount you currently have, you become more resilient. Wealth can fluctuate, but the qualities that built it remain. This internal security allows you to take bold yet thoughtful actions, knowing that even if circumstances change, your skills and mindset equip you to rebuild or grow again.

Ultimately, becoming who you must be to build wealth is not about becoming someone else entirely. It is about uncovering the part of you that is capable of thinking bigger, acting with discipline, and trusting in your ability to create value. This version of you already exists but may have been buried under years of conditioning and limitation. The work is to bring it to the surface, strengthen it, and let it guide your decisions consistently.

Part II. The Codes of Power and Leverage

Once you begin to see the hidden systems behind wealth, the next question arises: how do the elite actually use them? The answer lies in two forces that quietly shape every major financial breakthrough — power and leverage. These are not abstract ideas reserved for politicians or corporate executives. They are practical tools, available to anyone willing to understand how they work and apply them with intention.

Power, in this context, is not about domination or control over others. It is about influence — the ability to create options, open doors, and shape outcomes in your favor. Financial power allows you to negotiate better deals, attract partners, and secure opportunities that others never hear about. It begins internally, with clarity and confidence, and then extends outward through relationships, reputation, and the value you bring to the table.

Leverage is what turns that power into exponential results. It is the force that allows you to achieve more with less, multiplying effort, capital, and time. The wealthy do not simply work harder; they use leverage to amplify every move. This can take many forms — capital leverage through investments, skill leverage through specialized expertise, network leverage through connections, or system leverage through tools and technology. When these elements align, growth accelerates far beyond what linear effort could ever achieve.

Most people underestimate how deeply these forces influence everyday decisions. They believe success is purely the result of personal effort, yet behind every extraordinary result is a structure of leverage that magnifies that effort. Understanding this is a turning point. It reframes how you approach opportunities and challenges alike. Instead of asking, "How can I do this myself?" you begin asking, "What can I tap into that multiplies my outcome?"

This part of the book will guide you through these hidden codes. You will learn how to recognize where power truly comes from, how to cultivate it ethically, and how to apply leverage without overextending yourself. The goal is not to mimic the elite but to adopt the principles that allow them to achieve disproportionate results. When you integrate these lessons into your own strategy, you stop competing on the same level as everyone else and begin playing an entirely different game — one where your effort creates outcomes far larger than you imagined possible.

Chapter 3: Cracking the Code of Leverage

Financial Leverage: Debt, Assets, and Multiplication

One of the clearest distinctions between average earners and the wealthy is how they view leverage. For most people, debt is something to fear, assets are limited to a primary residence or retirement account, and multiplication is seen as unrealistic or reserved for the lucky few. The elite approach these concepts differently. They treat leverage as a strategic tool rather than a threat, recognizing that used wisely, it can accelerate wealth creation far beyond what personal income alone could achieve.

Leverage is essentially the ability to control more resources than you personally own. It allows you to amplify the results of your time, money, and decisions. When you borrow capital to invest in an appreciating asset, when you use one property to acquire another, or when you reinvest profits into scalable opportunities, you are practicing financial leverage. This concept is not new — it is the foundation of nearly every major fortune built throughout history — but its application requires understanding both its power and its risks.

Redefining Debt

The common narrative about debt is simple: avoid it at all costs. This message exists for good reason. Misused debt, especially consumer debt tied to depreciating purchases, traps millions in financial strain. High-interest credit cards, car loans, and lifestyle financing can erode wealth faster than almost any other factor. However, the wealthy differentiate between bad debt and productive debt.

Productive debt is borrowing that allows you to acquire or create assets that grow in value or generate income. Real estate investors, for example, routinely use mortgages not to buy liabilities, but to acquire properties that produce cash flow or appreciate over time. Entrepreneurs may take on strategic business loans to fund operations that will yield far greater returns than the cost of borrowing. The key is in the structure: using debt as a lever to create more value than it costs, rather than to fund consumption.

48

This mindset shift does not mean ignoring risk. In fact, managing risk becomes even more critical when using leverage. Wealthy individuals mitigate exposure through careful analysis, conservative cash flow projections, and contingency plans. They ensure that borrowed funds are tied to assets with intrinsic value, rather than speculative gambles. By treating debt as a tool instead of a trap, they unlock opportunities that remain invisible to those who fear it outright.

The Multiplying Effect of Assets

Assets are the engine that transforms leverage into lasting wealth. Income from a job is finite, but assets — when chosen wisely — can generate returns indefinitely. Real estate, equities, intellectual property, and business ownership all have the potential to create recurring income or appreciate over time. The wealthy focus less on saving for distant retirement and more on acquiring and growing assets that can support them indefinitely.

This approach shifts the timeline of financial freedom. Instead of waiting decades to enjoy the fruits of disciplined saving, insiders prioritize building portfolios of income-producing assets as early as possible. They reinvest earnings to acquire more assets, creating a compounding cycle. This is why fortunes tend to grow faster once they reach a certain threshold — the assets themselves begin to do the heavy lifting.

Even small-scale examples demonstrate this principle. Someone who owns a single rental property may reinvest the profits and equity growth into a second property, and then a third. Over time, what started as one modest investment can multiply into a portfolio that generates income far beyond what a single paycheck could provide. This is not a get-rich-quick tactic; it is a disciplined, structured approach that harnesses the multiplying effect of ownership.

Evaluating when to use leverage begins with clarity about your financial position and goals. Borrowing without a clear plan leads to unnecessary risk, but borrowing with a purpose aligned to well-researched opportunities can accelerate progress. The question is not simply "Can I borrow?" but "Will this borrowing create more value than it costs, and can I manage the downside if conditions change?" Answering this requires honest assessment of cash flow, market trends, and your own capacity to handle volatility.

A disciplined approach starts with stress testing your assumptions. Ask what happens if rents drop, markets correct, or timelines extend beyond what you expect. The wealthy prepare for these scenarios before committing capital. This preparation does not eliminate risk, but it prevents avoidable losses that come from overconfidence or neglecting worst-case outcomes. By approaching leverage conservatively, you position yourself to survive downturns and thrive in recoveries, which is when many fortunes quietly expand.

Multiplication happens when assets acquired through leverage generate returns that are reinvested into additional assets. This cycle can be slow at first, but momentum builds with each step. Profits from one property fund the next purchase. Equity from a growing business provides capital to invest in another venture. Dividends from a portfolio are reinvested rather than consumed. Over time, this creates a flywheel effect where growth accelerates independent of your direct labor.

One key discipline is resisting the temptation to overextend. Rapid growth can create the illusion of invincibility, leading to excessive borrowing or speculative decisions. History is full of examples where individuals built impressive empires only to lose them by ignoring risk controls. Sustainable wealth is built not on reckless expansion but on steady, calculated moves that prioritize long-term resilience over short-term excitement.

Balancing growth with stability often involves diversifying the forms of leverage you use. For example, combining real estate with other asset classes spreads risk across different market cycles. Leveraging networks or partnerships can amplify opportunities without relying solely on financial debt. Leveraging systems and technology can free your time and reduce operational strain, allowing you to focus on high-level strategy. In this way, leverage is not just about borrowing money; it is about using every available resource — capital, knowledge, relationships, and tools — to achieve exponential results.

The psychological aspect of leverage is equally important. Fear prevents many from using it, while overconfidence drives others to misuse it. Developing emotional discipline allows you to navigate between these extremes. This means being patient during times of growth, cautious during moments of hype, and opportunistic when others are retreating. It also means staying anchored in the principle that leverage should serve freedom, not create dependency. The purpose of multiplication is not to chase endless expansion but to create the space to live and work on your own terms.

Skill and Network Leverage

Wealth is rarely built in isolation. While financial capital is important, two other forms of leverage often prove even more powerful: skill and network. These are the multipliers that allow individuals to create extraordinary results without possessing vast resources at the start. Skills determine the value you can bring to opportunities, and networks determine the opportunities that even reach you. When these two elements combine, they create an upward spiral where ability and access reinforce each other, accelerating both personal and financial growth.

The Multiplier Effect of Skills

Skills are portable assets. They cannot be taken from you and often appreciate in value as markets evolve. A single high-leverage skill — such as negotiation, sales, coding, or strategic thinking — can transform your earning potential far beyond what hours worked alone could achieve. The wealthy understand this and invest heavily in building rare, valuable skills rather than solely relying on traditional credentials or titles.

High-leverage skills share certain characteristics. They either solve problems that few people can solve, create results that are highly valued, or can be applied repeatedly across multiple ventures. For example, a person skilled in negotiation can apply that ability to business deals, real estate purchases, partnership agreements, and even everyday financial decisions. The same skill compounds its value over time as it is used in multiple contexts.

Importantly, skills do not need to be mastered all at once. The most powerful approach is to stack complementary abilities. Someone who combines marketing expertise with copywriting and a basic understanding of analytics can create opportunities in entrepreneurship, consulting, or product development far greater than someone with a single isolated skill. This stacking principle explains why many successful individuals seem versatile: they have cultivated intersecting abilities that multiply one another's value.

Network as the Gateway to Opportunity

While skills increase the value you can provide, networks determine where you can provide it. Access to the right people opens doors that technical ability alone cannot unlock. Many of the most profitable opportunities — early investments, strategic partnerships, insider knowledge — circulate through trusted networks long before they appear to the general public.

This is not about exploiting connections but about cultivating mutual value. Strong networks are built on trust, reciprocity, and shared goals. When you help others achieve their objectives, you naturally create goodwill that leads to introductions and collaborations down the line. The wealthy invest time in nurturing these relationships, not just when they need something, but consistently over years.

Research in sociology highlights this principle. Mark Granovetter's concept of "weak ties," introduced in 1973, showed that people often access their most valuable opportunities through acquaintances rather than close friends. These weaker connections bridge different social circles, exposing you to information and prospects outside your immediate environment. By intentionally broadening and maintaining these connections, you increase the flow of opportunities that might otherwise remain invisible.

Combining Skills and Networks

The real leverage emerges when skills and networks intersect. A valuable skill without access can remain underutilized, while access without competence leads to missed opportunities. When you bring strong abilities into a network, you become a person of value, someone others are eager to collaborate with or recommend. This creates a compounding loop: the more value you provide, the more doors open; the more doors open, the more chances you have to apply and refine your skills.

Developing skill leverage begins with clarity about which abilities hold the highest potential return for your goals. Not all skills are equal. Some are widely available and easily replaced, while others are rare and command outsized rewards. The question to ask is, "Which skills create disproportionate value in the arenas I want to play in?" For someone entering entrepreneurship, this might be marketing or product development. For someone focused on investing, it might be financial analysis or deal structuring. By identifying skills that intersect personal strengths with market demand, you focus effort where growth will matter most.

Mastery of these abilities requires deliberate practice rather than passive learning. Consuming books, courses, or podcasts provides insight, but leverage emerges only when knowledge is applied repeatedly in real scenarios. This is why high performers actively seek feedback loops — opportunities to test, refine, and deepen their skills in environments where results matter. Each cycle of practice and reflection sharpens ability, turning competence into expertise and expertise into a competitive advantage that few can replicate.

Network leverage grows through similar intentionality. Rather than approaching networking as a numbers game, the focus is on quality and depth. Relationships built on authenticity and shared value endure far longer than superficial exchanges. Offering help without immediate expectation of return creates trust and goodwill, which in time translates into access and opportunities. The individuals who seem to have endless introductions and collaborations are often those who have consistently invested in others long before they needed anything themselves.

A practical way to nurture this dynamic is to view every interaction as an opportunity to plant seeds. A brief conversation, a helpful resource shared, or an introduction made on someone else's behalf can grow into meaningful connections months or even years later. Over time, these seeds create a web of trust that extends far beyond your immediate circle. When opportunities arise, people naturally think of those who have added value to their lives without strings attached.

The compounding effect becomes evident as skills and networks develop in tandem. As your abilities grow, you gain credibility within your circles. This credibility leads to more significant opportunities, which further refine and expand your skills. In parallel, as your network expands, you gain exposure to challenges and solutions that accelerate learning beyond what you could achieve alone. This synergy is why many people describe sudden breakthroughs in their careers as a mix of preparation and timing. In reality, these moments are rarely accidental. They are the culmination of years spent quietly building both competence and connection.

Maintaining this leverage requires consistent alignment with values and long-term vision. Skills can be misapplied, and networks can erode if treated purely as transactional tools. The individuals who sustain influence and opportunity are those who balance ambition with integrity. They recognize that reputation compounds just as much as expertise and that every decision contributes to how others perceive their reliability and character.

System Leverage: Build Once, Earn Repeatedly

One of the greatest distinctions between those who accumulate modest savings and those who build lasting wealth is how they approach their effort. Most people trade time for money on a recurring basis, starting from zero each day or each month. In contrast, those who achieve exponential results focus on building systems that continue to generate value long after the initial work is complete. This shift — from labor to leverage — is one of the most transformative changes in the journey toward financial independence.

System leverage is about creating structures that separate income from constant personal involvement. Instead of repeating the same tasks over and over, you design processes, assets, or platforms that work on your behalf. This could be a business that runs with minimal daily input, an automated investment strategy, or intellectual property that produces royalties long after it is created. Once built, these systems allow you to focus on higher-level strategy, pursue new opportunities, or simply reclaim time for the aspects of life that matter most.

Why Systems Outperform Effort

Effort alone has natural limits. You can only work so many hours in a day, and beyond a certain point, more effort leads to diminishing returns and burnout. Systems, on the other hand, scale. They allow results to multiply without requiring a matching increase in energy or time. A well-designed system creates predictability, efficiency, and consistency — three qualities that accelerate wealth creation.

Consider an online business that automates customer onboarding, billing, and product delivery. The initial setup might require significant energy, but once established, the system runs with minimal intervention. Each new customer adds revenue without adding proportional labor. The same principle applies to real estate portfolios with professional management, content that earns royalties, or investments structured for passive cash flow. The focus shifts from earning to building — from repeating to compounding.

This is why insiders prioritize creating systems early, even if they start small. They understand that every process automated or delegated frees mental bandwidth for higher-value decisions. They also recognize that systems compound over time: a single process might save an hour a week, but a dozen processes can reclaim entire days each month. This reclaimed time can then be invested in building the next layer of leverage, creating a snowball effect.

The Building Blocks of Effective Systems

Not all systems are created equal. For leverage to work, the structure must be repeatable, sustainable, and aligned with long-term goals. A system that requires constant tweaking or oversight is not truly freeing; it simply shifts where your attention is spent. The best systems are those that run predictably, with minimal maintenance, and continue delivering value long after the initial setup.

Building such systems often begins with mapping out repeatable tasks and identifying opportunities to automate or delegate them. Technology plays a central role here — from scheduling tools and customer relationship software to automated financial tracking and reporting. Equally important is documentation: clear processes ensure that tasks can be handed off without quality loss, whether to software, contractors, or future team members.

Identifying where to create systems begins with analyzing where your time and energy currently go. If certain actions repeat frequently or follow predictable steps, they are prime candidates for systemization. Even small processes — such as sending client updates, tracking expenses, or responding to inquiries — can be automated or delegated with significant cumulative impact. Over time, these incremental efficiencies free capacity to focus on creating higher-value assets rather than maintaining day-to-day operations.

When building systems, it is essential to start with clarity on desired outcomes. A system exists to achieve a specific result consistently. Define what success looks like before creating the process, whether it is predictable revenue, consistent client delivery, or accurate financial reporting. This clarity prevents overcomplication and ensures the system supports strategic goals rather than adding unnecessary complexity.

Scalability is another critical factor. A system that functions at a small scale but breaks under growth creates new problems instead of solving them.

Design with expansion in mind. For example, if you build an automated email sequence for a small audience, ensure it can handle ten times that volume without needing to be rebuilt. Similarly, a hiring or onboarding process should work just as well for your first team member as it will for your tenth. This foresight avoids costly restructuring later and allows growth to happen smoothly.

Systems also benefit from thoughtful integration. The most effective leverage occurs when multiple systems work together rather than in isolation. An example would be linking marketing automation with sales tracking and customer support. Each system serves its own function, but when connected, they create a seamless pipeline where data flows automatically and outcomes are easier to monitor. This interconnectedness reduces bottlenecks and provides a clearer picture of performance, enabling faster and more informed decisions.

Maintaining system leverage requires periodic review. Even well-designed processes can drift out of alignment as markets evolve or priorities change. A quarterly or biannual audit ensures that systems remain efficient and relevant. This does not mean constantly reinventing them, but rather making small adjustments to keep them optimized. The goal is to preserve freedom and scalability, not to create another layer of management that consumes attention.

A deeper benefit of system leverage is psychological. When recurring tasks are automated or delegated, mental bandwidth is freed for creativity and strategic thinking. This shift in focus allows you to explore new opportunities rather than being trapped in maintenance mode. It also reduces decision fatigue, as predictable processes minimize the number of small choices you face each day. Over time, this clarity compounds, making it easier to identify patterns, anticipate challenges, and act decisively.

Chapter 4: The Unwritten Rules of Power

Why Access Matters More Than Effort

Most people are taught from a young age that hard work is the ultimate path to success. The message is clear: put in the hours, push yourself further, and eventually the rewards will follow. While effort is undeniably important, it is not the defining factor in wealth creation. The missing element is access — access to information, opportunities, and networks that can multiply results far beyond what sheer labor could ever produce.

This explains why two individuals can work equally hard yet achieve vastly different outcomes. One spends years grinding without meaningful progress, while another, with the right introductions or knowledge, makes exponential leaps. The difference is not necessarily intelligence or dedication but proximity to opportunities that others never even see. Access acts as the bridge between potential and realization, transforming effort into leverage.

The Limits of Effort Alone

Effort, by its nature, is linear. It rewards consistency and discipline, but it is bound by the finite hours in a day. No matter how determined you are, there is a ceiling to what personal labor can produce. This is why many people who work tirelessly — sometimes harder than the wealthy — remain stuck in cycles of survival rather than advancement. Their output may be high, but it is applied in arenas with limited potential for scale.

This is not a moral failing but a structural one. The systems that govern wealth often reward access far more than exertion. For example, an individual who gains early access to a promising investment round can see life-changing returns with minimal ongoing effort. Someone else, equally hardworking but excluded from such opportunities, may never see those gains despite years of disciplined saving. The disparity is not about merit but about being positioned differently within the financial ecosystem.

Access as a Force Multiplier

Access multiplies the value of effort by opening doors that lead to higher-yield opportunities. A single introduction to the right mentor can shortcut years of trial and error. Gaining entry into specific professional or social circles can reveal deals, partnerships, and insights unavailable to the general public. This is not about favoritism but about information flow — the wealthiest individuals are often those who learn about opportunities early, when barriers to entry are low and upside potential is high.

The principle extends beyond money. Access to specialized knowledge accelerates skill development. Access to aligned communities fosters collaboration and shared growth. Even access to better tools and resources can dramatically change outcomes; the same amount of work applied with superior resources produces far greater results. Those who understand this shift their focus from solely working harder to strategically positioning themselves where their effort produces the highest return.

Barriers to Access

The challenge is that access is unevenly distributed. Many people assume that the doors to opportunity are permanently closed to them, reserved for those born into privilege or elite networks. While it is true that existing wealth and connections provide advantages, access is not fixed. It can be built, earned, and expanded over time through deliberate action. The first step is recognizing that it matters — that finding the right rooms to be in is as important as, if not more important than, the work you do once you are there.

Building access often begins incrementally. Attending industry events, contributing to communities, and consistently providing value are ways to establish credibility and forge relationships. Over time, these small steps compound, creating pathways into higher-level opportunities. The process requires patience and persistence but proves far more scalable than attempting to brute-force success through effort alone.

Creating access begins with clarity about the environments where high-value opportunities originate. These are often industry-specific events, mastermind groups, professional associations, or even informal communities where people exchange ideas and insights before they become widely known. Observing where conversations about upcoming trends, investments, or partnerships occur can reveal where you need to position yourself. Simply being present in these circles increases the likelihood of encountering opportunities that do not appear on public platforms.

The process is not about forcefully inserting yourself but about becoming valuable within those environments. The fastest way to gain trust in new circles is to contribute rather than consume. Offer insights, share resources, and look for ways to assist others without immediate expectation of return. Over time, this pattern of generosity positions you as someone people want to include in future conversations. In high-level networks, reputation is built not by self-promotion but by consistent demonstration of reliability and value.

One of the most overlooked elements of building access is patience. Relationships that lead to meaningful opportunities rarely develop overnight. They grow through repeated interactions and the gradual accumulation of trust. This is why consistency is more important than intensity. A single impressive meeting may spark interest, but it is regular follow-through and long-term engagement that transform acquaintances into allies. By approaching access as a lifelong strategy rather than a quick fix, you avoid the impatience that often derails authentic connection building.

Another key factor is aligning with shared values and goals. Access is not simply about proximity to power but about resonance with the people and opportunities you seek. When you operate from principles that others respect, doors open naturally. Those who try to gain entry through manipulation or pretense often find themselves excluded as soon as trust is tested. In contrast, when your ambitions align with mutual benefit, relationships deepen and lead to sustainable collaboration rather than transactional exchanges.

Access also grows through diversification. Limiting yourself to one circle or industry narrows the range of opportunities you encounter. Broadening exposure across different domains — technology, real estate, finance, creative industries — provides a wider view of where value is shifting. Many breakthroughs occur at the intersection of fields rather than within them. By cultivating relationships in multiple areas, you position yourself to spot patterns and possibilities that others miss.

The compounding nature of access becomes most apparent over time. Early efforts to attend events or build connections may seem slow or inconsequential, but each new relationship increases the surface area for opportunity. Introductions lead to further introductions, and insights gained in one context often apply in another. Eventually, opportunities begin finding you rather than the other way around. What once required deliberate searching becomes a steady flow of invitations, information, and options that accelerate progress far beyond what individual effort could achieve.

Understanding why access matters more than effort reframes how you approach your journey toward wealth. Hard work remains essential, but it must be paired with intentional positioning. By cultivating relationships, entering the right rooms, and earning trust within valuable networks, you ensure that your effort is directed toward opportunities capable of multiplying it. Over time, this combination of diligence and access creates an advantage that feels almost unfair to those still relying solely on hard work — yet it is built on principles anyone can learn and apply with consistency and integrity.

The Social Hierarchies of Wealth

Wealth is often discussed in terms of numbers — income, net worth, assets under management — but behind the figures lies a subtler structure: social hierarchies that influence how wealth is experienced, shared, and multiplied. These hierarchies exist in every society, shaping opportunities and perceptions in ways that are rarely acknowledged openly. Understanding them is not about reinforcing division but about recognizing the dynamics that govern access, influence, and upward mobility.

Social hierarchies of wealth are built on more than financial capital. They combine money with cultural awareness, networks, and influence. At the top are individuals who not only control significant resources but also set trends, shape narratives, and influence policy. Below them are layers of individuals who may be financially comfortable yet remain excluded from the circles where decisions and opportunities originate. The result is a multi-tiered system where not all wealth is perceived or treated equally.

The Layers of Visibility and Influence

The first layer consists of visible wealth — those whose success is recognized through lifestyle signals, public achievements, or high-profile positions. This layer often attracts admiration and envy, yet visibility does not always equate to power. Public figures can appear wealthy while lacking the deep influence or structural control held by less visible individuals. True power often resides in the second layer: quiet wealth. These are families and individuals who hold significant assets, often across generations, yet remain largely invisible to the public eye. Their influence flows through private networks, foundations, and ownership stakes that rarely make headlines.

A third layer consists of aspirational wealth — individuals rising quickly, often through entrepreneurship, high-demand skills, or early investment opportunities. They have crossed into financial abundance but are still building the networks and cultural capital required to move deeper into elite circles. Many at this stage face tension between outward success and inner access, appearing affluent while still navigating barriers to higher tiers of influence.

Understanding these layers matters because movement between them depends on more than increasing income. Cultural fluency, trust, and alignment with existing power structures often determine who gains entry into the next circle. Someone may achieve financial success yet remain excluded if they do not understand the unspoken rules of behavior, communication, and contribution that govern these hierarchies.

The Role of Cultural Capital

Cultural capital refers to the non-financial knowledge and behaviors that signal belonging within a particular group. This includes language, etiquette, shared experiences, and even the way people frame ideas or solve problems. Within wealthy circles, cultural capital can matter as much as net worth. Those who demonstrate understanding of these subtleties are welcomed into conversations and collaborations; those who do not may find doors quietly closed, regardless of financial standing.

For example, knowing how to navigate philanthropic events, investment discussions, or strategic partnerships often hinges on cultural cues rather than technical skill alone. This is not about superficial conformity but about developing an awareness of the environments you seek to enter. The more fluently you can move between contexts — from corporate boardrooms to grassroots initiatives — the more influence and opportunities you can unlock.

Understanding social hierarchies of wealth ultimately reframes how you approach your journey. Instead of chasing surface-level markers of success, you begin to focus on deeper layers: reputation, trust, and contribution. You learn to discern which circles align with your vision and which do not deserve your energy. Over time, this awareness allows you to move fluidly across different environments — from emerging opportunities to established institutions — without losing the core of who you are. The result is not just financial ascent but the cultivation of influence that can shape opportunities for others, creating a legacy that transcends personal gain.

Status Games vs. Real Power

The pursuit of wealth often tempts people into playing status games. These are contests centered on visible signals — luxury cars, designer clothing, exclusive memberships — rather than on the deeper foundations of influence and control. While status can attract attention and admiration, it rarely translates into lasting security or meaningful leverage. Real power, by contrast, operates quietly. It is built on ownership, access, and the ability to shape outcomes regardless of public recognition.

Understanding the difference between these two paths is essential. Many people waste years chasing appearances of success, believing they will lead to influence, only to discover that status without substance is fragile. Real power does not always look glamorous from the outside, but it is what ultimately drives decision-making, opportunity, and long-term wealth.

The Allure of Status

Status is seductive because it offers immediate feedback. A new car parked in the driveway or an expensive vacation shared online creates instant validation from peers. These visible markers suggest upward mobility and feed the human desire for social approval. For many, status becomes the primary measure of success — not because it brings true fulfillment, but because it is easy to display and widely understood.

The problem is that status games are inherently competitive. They require constant escalation to maintain their effect. Once a particular level of consumption becomes normalized, it loses its power to impress. This leads to an endless cycle of upgrading and performing for external validation, often funded by debt or at the expense of real wealth-building. People can appear rich while remaining financially vulnerable, prioritizing perception over actual security.

Status also misdirects focus. Instead of asking, "What creates enduring value?" the question becomes, "What will make me look successful right now?" This mindset pushes individuals toward short-term decisions, such as overextending on liabilities or chasing trends for recognition rather than carefully building assets that will compound quietly over time.

The Nature of Real Power

Real power is subtler and far more durable. It is the ability to influence outcomes regardless of outward appearances. A person with real power can access opportunities others cannot, shape decisions behind the scenes, and endure challenges without their foundation collapsing. This power comes from ownership of assets, control of systems, and trusted networks rather than public displays.

One hallmark of real power is its independence from constant validation. Quiet wealth does not need to announce itself because its influence is felt rather than seen. The families that have quietly owned land, businesses, or intellectual property for generations rarely appear on flashy social media feeds, yet they control resources that shape entire industries and communities. Their security comes from what they own, not from what others think they own.

Real power also expands options. It allows individuals to say no to opportunities that compromise values and to act from strategy rather than desperation. When you control assets or systems that generate recurring value, you gain time, flexibility, and the ability to make decisions with a long horizon. This stands in sharp contrast to status-driven pursuits, which often lock people into cycles of high spending and constant upkeep to maintain appearances.

Recognizing when you are caught in a status game often begins with examining your motivations. If a financial decision is driven primarily by how it will be perceived rather than how it serves your long-term vision, it is likely rooted in status. This could be an unnecessary upgrade, a purchase made to impress, or even a career move chosen for prestige rather than alignment. By pausing to ask whether the action creates enduring value or merely temporary approval, you gain clarity and protect yourself from cycles that drain resources without building real influence.

Refocusing on real power requires a shift in priorities from consumption to ownership. Instead of asking what you can buy to display success, the better question becomes what you can build or acquire that will continue producing value over time. This might mean prioritizing equity in a business rather than a higher salary, investing in intellectual property rather than luxury items, or cultivating relationships that open doors to new opportunities instead of ones that merely elevate social standing. Each choice compounds, gradually building a foundation of influence that no single purchase can replicate.

Avoiding status traps also means redefining what success looks like privately. Real power often grows in quiet phases, when external validation may be minimal. Those building meaningful assets frequently endure seasons where their work is misunderstood or overlooked. Patience becomes essential. The willingness to delay visible rewards in favor of compounding results separates those who achieve lasting freedom from those who burn out chasing appearances.

There is also a deeper emotional shift that occurs when you move from status to power. Status seeks to prove worth to others; power grows from knowing your worth internally. When your sense of identity is no longer tied to external approval, you gain the freedom to make unconventional choices, pursue long-term strategies, and act from conviction rather than comparison. This inner security is one of the greatest advantages in any wealth-building journey, allowing you to navigate volatility without being swayed by trends or public opinion.

Ethically applied, real power becomes generative rather than extractive. It allows you to create opportunities for others, influence systems for the better, and contribute to causes that extend beyond personal gain. This is where legacy begins. The individuals remembered for shaping industries or communities are rarely those who played the loudest status games; they are those who quietly built enduring structures and used their influence to elevate others.

Over time, the contrast between the two paths becomes clear. Status games consume resources and attention, leaving individuals perpetually striving for the next signal of worth. Real power, once established, multiplies resources and options, providing stability and influence that endures even through changing circumstances. The choice is not simply about wealth but about the life you want to create — one defined by constant performance for others or one rooted in quiet control and meaningful impact.

Chapter 5: Building Unfair Advantages

The Secrets Behind Opportunity Stacking

Most people view opportunities as isolated events — a job offer, an investment, a business idea — evaluating each one in isolation and deciding yes or no based on immediate potential. The wealthy view them differently. They see opportunities as building blocks, each one setting the stage for the next, compounding over time into something far greater than the sum of its parts. This principle is known as opportunity stacking, and it is one of the least understood yet most powerful strategies for creating exponential growth.

Opportunity stacking is about sequencing. Rather than chasing random chances, you intentionally align each move so it opens doors to bigger ones. This alignment turns seemingly small wins into stepping stones toward transformative outcomes. A modest skill learned today can position you for a collaboration tomorrow. A strategic partnership built in one industry can unlock entry into another. Each decision is evaluated not only for its direct payoff but for how it positions you for what comes next.

Why Stacking Creates Exponential Growth

Linear progress comes from isolated actions that produce limited outcomes. Exponential growth occurs when each action amplifies the potential of future ones. By stacking opportunities, you create momentum that compounds across time. This is why some individuals seem to rise rapidly — they are not just lucky, they are deliberate in how they connect one opportunity to another.

Consider someone who begins by freelancing in a niche market. Over time, they develop specialized expertise, which leads to consulting offers. Those consulting relationships expose them to investors who fund their first business. That business becomes a platform for partnerships in other ventures. At each stage, opportunities do not replace one another; they accumulate. Skills, networks, and resources gained from earlier steps continue to serve later ones, making each new move easier and more impactful than the last.

The Hidden Levers of Opportunity

Stacking opportunities requires more than seizing everything that appears. The key is selectivity. High performers learn to identify leverage points — opportunities that provide outsized benefits relative to effort and create pathways to additional doors. This often involves asking questions beyond the immediate reward: Will this introduce me to new people? Will it teach me skills transferable to other areas? Will it position me in a growing market?

Timing is equally important. Stacking works best when opportunities are pursued in a sequence that builds on itself rather than scattering attention. Jumping too quickly into unrelated ventures can dilute focus and prevent compounding. The wealthy are strategic in pacing their pursuits, often allowing one opportunity to mature before leveraging its results into the next. This patience does not slow them down; it ensures each step creates maximum lift for the next.

Building Stacks Across Different Dimensions

Opportunities stack across multiple dimensions: skills, capital, and relationships. Skills learned in one venture carry into future projects, making them easier and more profitable. Capital earned from an early win funds larger and riskier moves later. Relationships formed in one context often lead to introductions that open doors in entirely new arenas. The stacking effect is powerful because these dimensions compound together. A single opportunity might add value in all three areas, creating momentum far beyond what was visible at the start.

Designing an opportunity stack begins with clarity about the end state you want to reach. Without a vision, it is easy to collect opportunities that feel impressive in isolation but do not build toward a coherent outcome. Clarity allows you to filter options based on how well they align with your larger trajectory rather than chasing what seems immediately attractive. This approach prevents fragmentation and ensures each step compounds rather than competes with the next.

Foundational moves are often less glamorous than later opportunities but are critical for setting the stage. Developing a rare skill, building a strong reputation in a specific niche, or creating a modest but reliable income stream may not feel groundbreaking, yet these early moves create leverage that amplifies later decisions. The most resilient stacks are built on assets that continue providing value long after they are created — skills that remain relevant, relationships that deepen over time, and systems that scale without constant effort.

Recognizing patterns is essential for spotting stacking potential. Many opportunities follow similar cycles: learn, apply, gain credibility, expand. By understanding these patterns, you can anticipate what comes next and position yourself accordingly. For example, consulting for a company may reveal gaps that inspire you to create a product, which then attracts investors interested in scaling that solution. The first step sets the conditions for the second, and the third emerges naturally from the momentum already created.

Avoiding distractions is equally important. Not every opportunity that looks promising contributes to your stack. Some may pull you sideways into areas that consume energy without creating long-term alignment. This is why knowing your core direction matters: it gives you the ability to say no to good opportunities that are not the right opportunities. This discipline protects focus and ensures that each decision strengthens the foundation rather than scattering it.

As stacks mature, they begin to feed themselves. A single win in one domain creates visibility that draws new opportunities without active pursuit. Introductions come unprompted, collaborations form organically, and doors open that were once firmly shut. This stage can feel like luck to outsiders, but it is the predictable result of years spent aligning efforts in ways that compound rather than fragment.

The ultimate power of opportunity stacking lies in how it transforms time. Each aligned move reduces the effort required for the next, freeing energy to pursue higher-level strategies rather than constantly starting from zero. What once felt like climbing uphill begins to feel like momentum pulling you forward. With each layer added, you create not just wealth but optionality — the freedom to choose projects and directions based on vision rather than necessity.

Positioning Yourself Where the Money Flows

Financial success is not only about working hard or even working smart. It is also about being in the right place at the right time — positioning yourself where money, opportunities, and influence are already moving. This principle explains why two equally skilled individuals can experience radically different outcomes: one struggles to gain traction despite years of effort, while the other seems to attract opportunities with ease. The difference is not just talent but proximity to the flow of resources.

Money tends to move in patterns. It concentrates around industries experiencing growth, technologies driving innovation, and communities where talent and capital converge. By observing these patterns and positioning yourself accordingly, you reduce friction and increase the likelihood that your efforts will translate into results. This approach does not eliminate hard work, but it ensures that your work is amplified by momentum already in motion rather than fighting against it.

Understanding Money Currents

Every market has its own currents — areas where capital is entering and areas where it is leaving. These shifts are influenced by technology, cultural trends, policy changes, and evolving consumer behavior. For example, entire fortunes have been built by those who positioned themselves early in sectors like renewable energy, artificial intelligence, or e-commerce before mainstream adoption. In contrast, those clinging to declining industries often face diminishing returns, no matter how skilled or persistent they are. Identifying these currents requires curiosity and attentiveness. Rather than focusing solely on your immediate surroundings, pay attention to broader trends that signal where value is migrating. Where are companies investing heavily? Which skills are suddenly in high demand? What problems are emerging that were irrelevant five years ago but critical now? Answering these questions helps you anticipate where opportunity will be abundant rather than chasing it after it peaks.

The Power of Proximity

Once you identify where money is flowing, the next step is proximity. Being physically or virtually close to the epicenter of opportunity increases your access to information, people, and partnerships. This is why certain cities, industries, or even specific online communities become magnets for talent and capital. Proximity exposes you to conversations and insights that rarely appear in public channels, allowing you to act on opportunities sooner than those on the outside.

Proximity also builds credibility. When you operate within an environment where others are actively pursuing growth, you benefit from association. Shared context makes collaboration easier, and introductions happen naturally. This does not mean abandoning your current path entirely but rather finding ways to integrate into the ecosystems where your ambitions align with the flow of resources.

Strategic Alignment with Growth

Positioning yourself effectively requires alignment between your skills, values, and the opportunities in these high-flow areas. Simply chasing trends without alignment often leads to burnout or short-term wins that cannot be sustained. The goal is to identify intersections where your expertise solves problems emerging within growth industries or networks. This allows you to enter not as an outsider chasing hype but as a contributor bringing value. Embedding yourself where money flows begins with immersion. Observing trends from a distance can provide insights, but being present in the environments where decisions are made and deals are formed gives you a deeper understanding of unspoken dynamics. This presence allows you to witness emerging opportunities before they become obvious to the public. Conversations in these spaces often reveal problems yet to be solved, partnerships waiting to form, and shifts in direction that are not visible on the surface.

Immersion does not always require relocation or abandoning your current pursuits. It can be achieved through joining industry associations, attending conferences, or participating in digital communities where leaders and innovators exchange ideas. The key is consistent engagement rather than passive observation. By contributing meaningfully to these conversations, you begin to earn trust and visibility, which naturally leads to invitations into deeper circles of influence.

Another crucial step is learning to think like the people already positioned in these flows. This involves understanding not only what they do but why they do it — the priorities, challenges, and metrics that drive their decisions. When you can see opportunities through their lens, you become far more effective in identifying ways to add value. This shift in perspective transforms you from an outsider seeking advantage to a collaborator offering solutions, which is precisely what creates openings in tightly held networks.

Positioning also requires adaptability. Money flows are dynamic, often shifting faster than institutions or individuals can respond. A market that is lucrative today may become saturated tomorrow, while new frontiers emerge quietly in unexpected places. Staying relevant means cultivating a habit of ongoing learning and scanning for early signals of change. This is not about chasing every new trend but about refining your sense of timing — knowing when to enter, when to double down, and when to exit without emotional attachment.

The most strategic positioning combines timing with leverage. Once you have access to a flow of opportunity, the next step is to amplify your impact within it. This can mean building scalable systems, forming partnerships that expand reach, or reinvesting early wins into larger plays. The individuals who rise fastest within growth sectors are those who not only identify the currents but learn how to multiply their exposure to them without spreading themselves too thin.

Over time, this approach shifts your relationship with opportunity. Instead of scrambling to find where money is moving, you become part of the ecosystems that generate it. You develop a reputation that attracts invitations rather than requiring constant pursuit. Opportunities begin to stack, each new one building on the credibility and relationships established by previous ones. What feels accidental to outsiders — being in the right place at the right time — is the product of deliberate positioning, cultivated over months and years.

The ultimate reward of this strategy is freedom. When you are positioned where value naturally concentrates, you no longer rely on luck or endless hustle to move forward. You gain the ability to choose projects and partnerships that align with your vision, knowing that the environment itself is working in your favor.

The Hidden Value of Asymmetry

One of the most overlooked principles in wealth creation is asymmetry. In simple terms, asymmetry describes situations where the potential upside of an action is far greater than its downside. These opportunities allow you to risk little while standing to gain significantly, creating disproportionate rewards compared to the resources invested. Understanding and seeking asymmetry is a key reason why some individuals consistently outperform others despite having similar levels of capital, skill, or time.

Most people approach decisions symmetrically. They expect proportional returns for proportional effort: work twice as hard, earn twice as much. While this mindset feels intuitive and safe, it limits growth. Asymmetry breaks this pattern. It allows for outcomes where a small bet, made strategically, can lead to transformative gains. This is not about gambling or reckless risk-taking; it is about identifying scenarios where the worst-case outcome is manageable but the best-case outcome is life-changing.

Recognizing Asymmetric Opportunities

Asymmetric opportunities often appear unremarkable at first. They might involve small investments of money, time, or energy that have the potential to unlock exponential outcomes. For example, learning a high-leverage skill like copywriting or negotiation may require a modest initial commitment but can create disproportionate advantages across every future career or business venture. Similarly, building relationships in an emerging industry can cost little upfront but later grant access to opportunities that others cannot reach.

Financial investments are another clear example. Early participation in a promising venture — whether it is a startup, a new market trend, or an undervalued asset — carries limited initial exposure but significant potential reward if the venture succeeds. The wealthy excel at spotting these situations, not because they take wild risks, but because they structure their actions to minimize downside while preserving access to unlimited upside.

Why Most People Miss Asymmetry

The reason most individuals fail to capitalize on asymmetry is psychological. Human nature is biased toward avoiding loss rather than seeking gain. This leads to overestimating the risks of small bets while underestimating the opportunity cost of inaction. As a result, people cling to safe but limited paths, missing the quiet opportunities that could have transformed their trajectory.

Cultural conditioning also plays a role. Traditional advice emphasizes predictable returns: steady jobs, fixed salaries, and cautious investments. While this provides stability, it rarely leads to breakthroughs. Those who understand asymmetry operate differently. They look for unfair advantages — information others overlook, timing others misunderstand, and leverage others ignore — that allow them to achieve disproportionate results without proportional exposure.

Building an Asymmetric Lens

Shifting toward an asymmetric mindset requires a new way of evaluating decisions. Instead of asking, "What is the average return?" you begin asking, "What is the worst that could happen, and can I handle it? What is the best that could happen, and is it worth pursuing?" This framing highlights opportunities where the downside is tolerable but the upside is extraordinary. Over time, making repeated asymmetric decisions creates a portfolio of bets where even a small number of wins can outweigh numerous small losses.

Applying this principle begins with learning to scan for opportunities others dismiss. Often, asymmetric plays hide in plain sight because they appear too small or too unconventional to attract broad attention. A side project that develops into a business, an early investment in a niche technology, or a relationship with an overlooked innovator can later become the defining leverage point in someone's career. The key is paying attention to areas where barriers to entry are low but the potential for growth is significant if the bet succeeds.

To act on these opportunities effectively, you must structure them to minimize downside. This can involve setting clear limits on what you are willing to risk — a defined budget, a fixed amount of time, or a specific milestone for reassessment. By capping potential losses, you create psychological safety that allows you to participate without fear of catastrophic failure. The wealthy apply this principle repeatedly: they diversify across multiple asymmetric bets, knowing that even if several fail, a single win can more than compensate for the rest.

Patience is critical when pursuing asymmetry. Transformative opportunities rarely unfold on predictable timelines. It can take years for a skill to translate into influence, for an investment to appreciate, or for a connection to mature into a partnership. Impatience leads many to abandon positions just before they begin to compound. Viewing asymmetric decisions as long-term plays — seeds planted for future harvest — allows you to endure the quiet phases before visible results appear.

An important nuance is that asymmetry is not limited to financial opportunities. It applies equally to personal growth and positioning. Reading a single book that reshapes your worldview, reaching out to one mentor who changes the course of your career, or taking one deliberate step into a growing industry can all have disproportionate impact compared to the modest effort they require. The common thread is recognizing where a small input has the potential to unlock cascading benefits across multiple dimensions of your life.

Developing an instinct for asymmetry requires repetition and reflection. Each decision teaches you to evaluate upside and downside more accurately, to spot patterns in timing and context, and to trust the compounding effect of small, calculated risks. Over time, this lens reshapes how you approach everything from career moves to investments to relationships. You begin to prioritize actions that open multiple future paths rather than those that lock you into a single outcome.

The greatest advantage of this approach is that it changes the scale of what becomes possible. When you rely solely on symmetrical exchanges — trading time for money, effort for predictable reward — growth is capped by the limits of your own capacity. Asymmetric decisions, by contrast, tap into leverage that multiplies results far beyond personal effort. One well-placed action can alter the trajectory of years. A single insight can generate opportunities that ripple outward indefinitely.

By seeking, structuring, and compounding asymmetric opportunities, you step into a different game than the one most people play. Instead of grinding for incremental gains, you position yourself for infrequent but transformative breakthroughs. Over a lifetime, these rare moments of disproportionate reward shape outcomes far more than the steady, linear progress others pursue. Mastering this principle does not eliminate risk, but it aligns you with the hidden dynamics that drive extraordinary wealth and influence.

Part III. Mastering the Insider Playbook

By now, you have explored the foundations that set insiders apart and uncovered the hidden dynamics of power, leverage, and positioning. But knowing these principles is only the beginning. What separates those who understand the game from those who truly master it is their ability to apply these insights deliberately and consistently, turning them into a personal playbook for navigating wealth creation.

The insider playbook is not a rigid set of tactics. It is a way of thinking, a lens that changes how you see opportunities and risks. It allows you to anticipate moves before they happen, to read patterns others overlook, and to align your actions with forces already shaping the financial landscape. This shift in perspective transforms every decision — from where you spend your time to how you deploy capital — into part of a larger strategy rather than a series of disconnected choices.

Mastering this approach also demands discipline. The temptation to chase quick wins or mimic surface-level behaviors of the wealthy is strong, but insiders know the real advantage lies in patient, strategic execution. They invest in building credibility, cultivating relationships, and creating systems that compound over time. Their success is rarely about a single breakthrough; it is about a series of deliberate moves that stack to create seemingly effortless momentum.

This part of the book will focus on turning these principles into action. You will explore how to cultivate insider awareness, design strategies that maximize leverage without sacrificing integrity, and position yourself for opportunities that accelerate rather than exhaust you. The goal is not to imitate someone else's path but to develop the clarity and confidence to craft your own — one that aligns with your strengths, values, and long-term vision for wealth and freedom.

Approach these chapters with intention. The insights here are most powerful when internalized, not just understood. As you read, consider where these strategies intersect with your own life, where you can begin applying them immediately, and where patience is required for deeper positioning. This is where theory becomes practice, and where understanding the hidden side of wealth turns into living it.

Chapter 6: Wealth Barriers You Don't See

Cultural and Psychological Money Blocks

For many people, the greatest obstacles to building wealth are not external circumstances but internal beliefs. These beliefs, often inherited from family, community, or culture, shape how we view money and what we believe is possible for us. They operate quietly, influencing decisions in ways we rarely notice, yet their impact can be profound — limiting opportunities, sabotaging progress, and keeping us from stepping into financial potential even when tools and strategies are available.

The Cultural Inheritance of Money Beliefs

Every culture carries narratives about wealth. Some teach that money is scarce and must be hoarded. Others glorify self-sacrifice and view financial ambition with suspicion. Many religious or philosophical traditions elevate modesty and warn against materialism, which can create tension for individuals striving for financial growth. None of these perspectives are inherently wrong, but when unexamined, they can create invisible barriers. Family dynamics deepen these narratives. Growing up in an environment where money was a source of stress or conflict often imprints the idea that wealth is unsafe or unattainable. Children raised hearing statements like "We can't afford that," "Money doesn't grow on trees," or "Rich people are greedy" absorb these beliefs long before they are capable of questioning them. As adults, they may unconsciously replicate these attitudes, even while consciously striving for a better financial reality.

Psychological Patterns That Sabotage Wealth

Beyond cultural influences, personal psychological patterns often play a role. One of the most common is fear — fear of failure, fear of judgment, or even fear of success. Fear of failure can prevent people from taking calculated risks, while fear of judgment leads them to downplay ambition to avoid criticism. Fear of success, though less obvious, is equally powerful; it arises from anxiety about the responsibilities and expectations that accompany greater wealth.

Another block is self-worth. If someone secretly believes they do not deserve abundance, they will unconsciously reject opportunities or self-sabotage when success arrives. This can manifest as undercharging for services, hesitating to negotiate, or procrastinating on actions that would lead to advancement. Low self-worth and money struggles often reinforce each other, creating a cycle where financial limitations seem to confirm internal doubts.

Scarcity mentality is another significant barrier. It fosters a zero-sum view of the world, where someone else's gain feels like your loss. This mindset makes it difficult to collaborate, invest, or pursue bold opportunities because every action is weighed against a fear of depletion. Scarcity-driven individuals often cling to security at the expense of growth, missing asymmetric opportunities that could dramatically shift their trajectory.

The Role of Social Conditioning

Society reinforces these blocks through subtle but persistent messaging. Media glorifies overnight success stories while downplaying the years of preparation behind them, creating unrealistic expectations and frustration when results do not appear quickly. At the same time, there is a quiet disdain for wealth in many circles, where success is met with suspicion rather than curiosity. These conflicting signals breed confusion: people are encouraged to desire wealth but criticized when they pursue it too visibly.

Breaking free from this conditioning requires awareness and conscious choice. You cannot transform what you cannot name. By examining the beliefs you inherited and questioning whether they still serve you, you begin to reclaim power over your financial story.

The first step in dismantling these barriers is awareness. Identifying the specific narratives you carry about money creates space to challenge them. This often requires honest reflection: What messages about wealth did you hear growing up? How do you feel when you think about financial success? Are there patterns in your behavior — like avoiding opportunities or feeling uncomfortable discussing money — that trace back to these beliefs? Naming the root of the block turns an unconscious limitation into something you can consciously work through.

81

Once awareness is established, reframing becomes possible. Reframing is the practice of replacing limiting interpretations with empowering ones. If you were taught that seeking wealth is selfish, reframing might involve recognizing that financial stability allows you to provide for your family, support meaningful causes, and contribute more fully to your community. If you were conditioned to believe money is scarce, reframing means adopting the view that value can be created and expanded, rather than competed for. This shift does not ignore reality but transforms your approach to it, turning fear-driven decisions into opportunity-driven ones.

Healing self-worth is another critical element. Building wealth is not only about strategy; it is also about believing you deserve the results of your efforts. Practices like setting clear boundaries, celebrating small wins, and acknowledging personal growth reinforce self-trust and confidence. Over time, these habits counteract internalized narratives of unworthiness and create a foundation from which bold financial moves feel natural rather than reckless.

Practical action supports psychological change. Taking even small steps toward financial goals — opening an investment account, asking for a raise, starting a side project — provides evidence that challenges old narratives. Each action reinforces the belief that progress is possible, gradually replacing fear with competence. This momentum compounds; as confidence grows, so does willingness to pursue larger opportunities.

Community also plays a pivotal role in overcoming cultural and psychological blocks. Surrounding yourself with people who view wealth creation as positive and attainable reshapes what feels normal. Conversations about strategy, growth, and success become sources of inspiration rather than shame. In this environment, ambition is celebrated, not criticized, and new standards of possibility emerge.

Addressing these blocks is not about discarding values like humility or generosity but about removing the distortions that equate financial aspiration with greed or moral compromise. True wealth aligns with integrity, allowing you to create abundance without abandoning what matters most. When internal resistance dissolves, you can approach financial growth with clarity and calm, no longer battling subconscious fears that sabotage your progress.

Ultimately, dismantling cultural and psychological money blocks transforms wealth-building from a constant uphill struggle into a more fluid process. The energy once spent resisting opportunities or second-guessing decisions becomes available for creativity, strategy, and meaningful contribution. Freed from inherited limitations, you can design a financial path that reflects your highest potential — one where prosperity is not only possible but sustainable, rooted in both capability and self-belief.

The Hidden Cost of Comfort and Safety

Most people spend their lives seeking comfort and safety. These goals are celebrated as signs of success: a stable job, a predictable income, a home free from risk or uncertainty. Yet what is rarely discussed is the quiet cost of this pursuit. Comfort, while soothing, often creates stagnation. Safety, while necessary, can become a prison when it prevents bold action. The very conditions designed to protect us can end up limiting the growth, freedom, and wealth we desire most.

Comfort is seductive because it feels like relief from struggle. After years of striving, finally reaching a point where bills are paid, routines are predictable, and life feels manageable seems like the reward. But comfort quickly becomes self-reinforcing. The more familiar life becomes, the harder it is to challenge the status quo. New opportunities, which often require discomfort, begin to feel threatening rather than exciting. In this way, comfort lulls people into maintaining a life far smaller than what they are capable of creating.

Safety operates in a similar way. While it is wise to avoid reckless risk, many confuse safety with avoiding all uncertainty. True safety does not exist — markets shift, industries evolve, and unexpected events can disrupt even the most carefully planned lives. Yet the illusion of safety keeps people tied to situations that feel secure in the short term but are eroding potential in the long term. Staying in a job that offers stability but little growth, holding onto cash instead of investing, or avoiding new ventures for fear of failure are common expressions of this mindset.

The Psychological Trap of Comfort

Human beings are wired to seek predictability. Our nervous systems interpret the unknown as potential danger, triggering hesitation even when the opportunity is positive. Over time, this instinct creates a subtle psychological trap: we begin to equate familiar with safe and unfamiliar with risky. This bias explains why people often cling to environments they dislike simply because they know what to expect.

The trap deepens when comfort is combined with incremental rewards. A steady paycheck, annual raises, or occasional promotions provide just enough satisfaction to prevent serious change. This creates what psychologists call a "variable reward cycle," where small but inconsistent benefits keep people engaged without ever delivering transformative outcomes. In financial terms, this translates to decades of linear growth while exponential opportunities pass by unnoticed.

How Safety Can Become Expensive

Ironically, playing it safe often comes with hidden costs. Avoiding investments to protect capital can mean losing purchasing power to inflation. Declining opportunities to preserve stability can result in missing entire waves of market growth. Even in personal development, prioritizing safety can lead to stagnation that erodes confidence and adaptability over time. What feels safe in the moment can, in the long run, become one of the riskiest choices of all.

Breaking free from this cycle begins with redefining what safety actually means. Real safety does not come from avoiding risk altogether but from building resilience. When you develop skills, diversify income streams, and create systems that can withstand volatility, you are no longer dependent on a single source of security. This kind of safety allows you to take calculated risks without fear of total collapse, because even if one venture fails, your foundation remains strong.

Gradually expanding your tolerance for discomfort is essential. Most people think they must leap from comfort into chaos, but sustainable growth happens in stages. Deliberately stepping outside familiar routines — speaking up in rooms where you would normally stay quiet, investing in learning a new skill, or testing a side project while maintaining your current income — conditions your mind and body to handle uncertainty. Each small step builds confidence, making larger moves feel less intimidating over time.

Reframing risk is equally powerful. Rather than viewing risk as something to avoid, see it as the price of opportunity. Every meaningful breakthrough carries some level of uncertainty, but not all risks are equal. A well-researched investment, a carefully chosen business venture, or a career shift into a growing industry can carry far greater upside than downside if approached strategically. The question shifts from "Is this risky?" to "What is the worst that could happen, and can I handle it? What is the best that could happen, and is it worth pursuing?"

Another practical strategy is setting defined safety nets. This might involve maintaining an emergency fund, developing multiple streams of income, or building a skill set that remains valuable regardless of market changes. These safeguards allow you to take bold action without reckless exposure. The presence of a safety net reduces anxiety and frees mental bandwidth for strategic thinking rather than constant worry.

Equally important is challenging the cultural conditioning that equates comfort with success. It is easy to internalize messages that the end goal of financial progress is relaxation, early retirement, or perpetual ease. While rest and recovery matter, a life built entirely around comfort tends to shrink over time. Humans are wired for growth and contribution; without new challenges, even the most comfortable circumstances eventually feel hollow. Recognizing this truth reframes discomfort as a sign of progress rather than a signal to retreat.

Over time, choosing growth over comfort leads to compounding rewards. Each bold move not only creates new opportunities but also strengthens your ability to navigate uncertainty. This combination of skill, resilience, and confidence is what separates those who remain stuck in safe mediocrity from those who ascend to lasting freedom and influence.

How Society Programs You to Stay Average

From childhood, most people are taught to follow a path that promises security and predictability. Go to school, get good grades, find a stable job, and save for retirement. On the surface, this advice seems reasonable — it offers a straightforward formula for living without major financial disasters. Yet beneath this structure lies an implicit program designed not to help you rise to your highest potential, but to keep you comfortably average. It rewards compliance over creativity, predictability over ambition, and safety over innovation.

The Blueprint of Compliance

Education is one of the earliest places this programming begins. Traditional schooling is structured to produce conformity rather than independent thinking. Students are graded on how well they follow instructions, memorize facts, and fit into a standardized system. Rarely are they taught to question the system itself, identify opportunities outside the curriculum, or develop skills that lead to unconventional success. Those who excel at compliance are celebrated, while those who think differently are often labeled as disruptive or unfocused.

This conditioning continues into higher education and the workforce. Career paths are framed as ladders, with success measured by incremental promotions rather than leaps into new paradigms. The idea of starting your own business, challenging industry norms, or pursuing high-risk, high-reward ventures is subtly discouraged in favor of climbing a predefined hierarchy. The system benefits from this arrangement: it ensures a steady supply of workers willing to exchange their time for wages, maintaining the stability of institutions that rely on predictability.

The Illusion of Opportunity

Modern society reinforces this programming by offering carefully curated illusions of choice. Consumer culture celebrates freedom — the freedom to choose between endless brands, lifestyles, and entertainment — while leaving the deeper structures of wealth creation untouched. People feel empowered when choosing what to buy, yet remain unaware of how little influence they have over the systems that determine where money flows.

Media plays a central role in sustaining this illusion. Success stories are often presented as exceptional rather than replicable. The wealthy are portrayed as either unreachable icons or morally questionable figures, subtly discouraging aspiration. At the same time, entertainment normalizes average living, reinforcing the idea that steady work, modest consumption, and occasional indulgence are the peak of what most people can hope for.

Social Pressure and the Fear of Standing Out

Beyond institutions and media, social pressure powerfully enforces average behavior. Humans are wired for belonging, and stepping outside accepted norms can trigger discomfort both for the individual and those around them. When someone begins to pursue extraordinary goals — whether building a business, investing aggressively, or simply questioning traditional financial advice — they often face skepticism or even ridicule from peers and family.

This resistance is rarely malicious. It stems from fear and misunderstanding. People project their own insecurities when they see someone breaking away from the norm. Rather than confronting their doubts about what is possible, they try to pull others back into familiar territory. This social gravity keeps many ambitious individuals from fully committing to their potential, convincing them to settle for incremental improvements rather than bold transformation.

This programming is reinforced by deeply ingrained psychological mechanisms. One of the most powerful is loss aversion — the tendency to fear losing what we already have more than we value gaining something new. This bias makes people cling to jobs, habits, and routines that feel safe, even when better opportunities are available. Another is social proof. When everyone around you follows the same script, deviation feels risky, even if logic suggests otherwise. We assume that if the majority is doing something, it must be the right thing, forgetting that the majority outcome is rarely extraordinary wealth or freedom.

The result is a cycle of quiet resignation. People learn to aim for goals that are acceptable rather than transformative: a steady paycheck, a mortgage, a comfortable retirement. Anything beyond that seems excessive or unrealistic. This belief system is rarely questioned because it is woven into the very structure of everyday life. Schools teach it, workplaces reward it, and communities normalize it. It feels natural because it is everywhere.

Breaking out of this programming begins with awareness. You cannot reject what you cannot see. The moment you realize that many of your beliefs about money and success were inherited rather than chosen, you gain the ability to examine them critically. Are they serving you, or are they keeping you stuck? This simple question opens the door to a deeper evaluation of the assumptions guiding your decisions.

From there, it becomes essential to seek alternative perspectives. Exposure to people who operate outside the average path reshapes what you believe is possible. Reading biographies of unconventional achievers, joining communities where ambition is celebrated rather than dismissed, or learning directly from mentors who have broken free from traditional systems creates a new reference point. What once felt unattainable begins to feel achievable, not because the world changes, but because your internal map expands.

Another key shift is redefining success on your own terms. The programming to stay average thrives on comparison — measuring yourself against societal milestones like home ownership, job titles, or retirement savings benchmarks. While these markers may provide temporary comfort, they rarely lead to fulfillment. True success emerges when you align your financial goals with your values, vision, and desired lifestyle rather than chasing approval or conformity. This alignment not only fuels motivation but also inoculates you against the criticism and doubt that often accompany unconventional choices.

Escaping average does not mean rejecting stability entirely. It means building stability in ways that empower bold action rather than restrict it. This might involve creating a financial cushion that allows you to pursue higher-risk opportunities, developing multiple income streams to reduce dependence on a single employer, or mastering skills that give you leverage in any market. Safety becomes a platform for growth rather than a reason to avoid it.

The deeper reward of breaking free from this societal program is not just financial. It is psychological liberation — the realization that you are not limited to the script handed to you. When you stop living by default and begin living by design, you access a level of creativity and confidence that average thinking cannot provide. Over time, this mindset compounds. Each bold decision expands your sense of what is possible, creating a virtuous cycle that pulls you further from mediocrity and closer to the life you were capable of all along.

Chapter 7: The Insider's Playbook on Assets

The Real Asset Classes That Build Lasting Wealth

Most people think of assets only in terms of what they can see: a house, a car, a savings account, maybe a retirement plan. While some of these can play a role in financial security, they are rarely the drivers of lasting wealth. The wealthy think about assets differently. They see them as vehicles for leverage, freedom, and compounding value over time. Understanding these real asset classes — the ones that quietly but consistently generate wealth across generations — is essential to building a financial foundation that endures.

Tangible Assets with Productive Value

Real estate is one of the most time-tested vehicles for wealth building. Not all property qualifies, though. A primary residence, while valuable, does not necessarily produce income or grow wealth beyond market appreciation. Productive real estate — rental properties, commercial spaces, land with development potential — creates cash flow while appreciating in value. This dual function is what makes it so powerful: it pays you now and builds long-term equity simultaneously.

Ownership of productive real estate also offers unique tax advantages, such as depreciation deductions and the ability to leverage financing to amplify returns. While it requires management and carries risk, it is one of the few asset classes where ordinary individuals can use other people's money — via mortgages or partnerships — to control appreciating assets. The result is a powerful combination of income and growth that compounds steadily over time.

Business Ownership and Equity

Another cornerstone of lasting wealth is equity in businesses. Unlike wages, which stop when you stop working, equity creates a share in something that continues generating value. This could be ownership in your own company, shares in private ventures, or stakes in publicly traded businesses through the stock market. The key is understanding that real wealth is rarely built by renting out your time but by owning systems that operate beyond your personal labor.

For many self-made wealthy individuals, building or investing in businesses provides the highest return on effort. A single successful venture can eclipse decades of salary income, not only in financial terms but also in freedom and control. Equity ownership benefits from compounding growth and, in some cases, liquidity events such as acquisitions or public offerings, which can transform modest investments into generational wealth.

Intellectual Property and Creative Assets

In the modern economy, intellectual property is an increasingly valuable asset class. Books, patents, software, courses, and media content can generate royalties or licensing income long after the initial work is completed. This is another form of building once and earning repeatedly — a principle that separates those who rely on active income from those who enjoy passive or semi-passive cash flow.

What makes intellectual property especially powerful is its scalability. A book can sell millions of copies without additional printing costs from the creator's side in digital formats. A piece of software can serve thousands of customers with minimal incremental expense. This scalability allows for disproportionate returns compared to the effort required to create the asset, especially when paired with strong distribution systems.

Financial Instruments That Compound

Traditional financial assets — such as stocks, bonds, and index funds — remain core components of wealth-building when used strategically. While they may not offer the outsized returns of entrepreneurship or early real estate plays, they provide liquidity, diversification, and a reliable compounding effect over time. The difference between average and extraordinary results often lies in consistency: reinvesting dividends, holding through market cycles, and understanding the fundamentals of long-term growth rather than chasing trends.

The most resilient wealth strategies emerge from combining these asset classes rather than relying on a single one. Real estate provides stability and tangible value. Business equity drives high-growth potential and control over income. Intellectual property and creative assets add scalability, often requiring less ongoing involvement once built. Financial instruments balance the portfolio, offering liquidity and compounding returns over time. Together, they create a system where strengths in one area compensate for temporary weaknesses in another.

Diversification, however, does not mean spreading yourself thin across unrelated ventures. The wealthy build assets that complement each other. A business might generate cash flow used to acquire real estate, while the real estate provides collateral for further expansion. Profits from intellectual property could be invested into index funds or dividend-paying stocks, ensuring stability as the creative work continues to generate income. This interconnected approach creates layers of security and opportunity that reinforce each other rather than compete for attention.

Time horizon is another factor that distinguishes lasting wealth from short-term gains. Each asset class operates on a different rhythm. Financial markets may offer liquidity but require patience to ride out volatility. Real estate compounds steadily but demands upfront capital and ongoing management. Business ventures can scale rapidly yet carry higher risk and emotional investment. Recognizing these timelines allows you to balance quick wins with long-term plays, maintaining momentum without sacrificing sustainability.

A critical but often overlooked asset class is relationships. While not recorded on a balance sheet, the quality of your network determines access to deals, insights, and partnerships that multiply the value of every other asset. The wealthiest individuals prioritize cultivating trust and reciprocity, knowing that opportunities often flow through people rather than platforms. Relationships with mentors, peers, and collaborators provide perspectives that accelerate learning and prevent costly mistakes, serving as a quiet but powerful form of leverage.

Knowledge itself functions as an asset when treated intentionally. Skills that increase earning potential, insights that identify undervalued opportunities, and frameworks that guide decision-making compound over time in much the same way as capital. The wealthiest individuals often reinvest in their own education, not because they lack resources, but because they understand that sharper thinking leads to better strategies and higher returns. In this way, personal growth becomes inseparable from financial growth.

Building lasting wealth is not about chasing every trend or mastering every asset class at once. It is about sequencing intelligently — mastering one pillar at a time, reinvesting gains into the next, and ensuring each layer strengthens the foundation rather than destabilizing it. A career may begin with active income that funds savings, which evolves into real estate or business ownership, which then creates surplus for intellectual property or market investments. Over years, these decisions form a web of assets that continue to grow long after the initial effort is complete.

The deeper insight is that lasting wealth depends less on any single strategy and more on the ability to think like an owner across multiple domains. Ownership of cash-flowing assets, scalable ideas, and meaningful relationships creates freedom far beyond financial security. It provides influence, resilience, and the capacity to pursue opportunities on your own terms. This mindset — prioritizing assets that endure and compound — is what transforms financial success into a legacy capable of spanning generations.

How the Rich Structure Their Portfolios

The portfolios of wealthy individuals look very different from the average investor's. While most people focus on basic savings accounts, a retirement fund, and perhaps some real estate, the rich treat their portfolios as dynamic ecosystems designed to balance growth, cash flow, and resilience. Their approach is less about finding a single perfect investment and more about creating harmony between different types of assets, each serving a specific purpose in both protecting and expanding wealth.

Core Principles Behind Wealthy Portfolios

One defining principle is diversification, but not in the way it is often misunderstood. Average investors tend to diversify by spreading small amounts across various mutual funds or stocks, aiming simply to reduce risk. The wealthy diversify by function rather than just by category. They hold assets that serve distinct roles: some generate income, others appreciate over time, some hedge against inflation, and others provide liquidity for new opportunities. This functional approach ensures that their portfolios perform well across different economic cycles.

Another guiding principle is ownership. Wealthy individuals prioritize assets they can control or influence rather than relying entirely on market movements. This might mean owning real estate, holding equity in private businesses, or creating intellectual property. Control provides flexibility: they can improve the asset, restructure it, or leverage it to unlock additional opportunities. Public market investments may still play a role, but they are rarely the sole focus.

Tax efficiency is also central to how the rich structure their wealth. They view every investment through the lens of after-tax returns rather than headline numbers. This means strategically using vehicles like trusts, holding companies, and tax-advantaged accounts, as well as timing sales and reinvestments to minimize liabilities. By reducing tax drag, they allow compounding to work more effectively, growing wealth faster without taking on additional risk.

Balancing Growth and Stability

Wealthy portfolios typically blend high-growth and stable assets. Growth-oriented components might include stakes in private companies, venture capital funds, or emerging markets. These carry higher risk but also the potential for extraordinary returns. Stability comes from holdings like income-producing real estate, bonds, or blue-chip dividend stocks, which provide predictable cash flow and act as ballast during volatile periods.

This balance allows the wealthy to remain opportunistic without jeopardizing their foundation. When markets decline, their stable assets cover living expenses and free them from panic selling. When opportunities arise, they have liquidity or leverage to act decisively. This dual approach — security combined with flexibility — enables them to withstand economic shocks while continuing to grow their net worth.

Alternative Investments and Hidden Leverage

Another hallmark of wealthy portfolios is the inclusion of alternative investments. These can range from private equity and hedge funds to commodities, art, and even farmland. While not all alternatives are appropriate for every investor, they often provide returns that are uncorrelated with traditional markets, enhancing resilience.

Leverage is used selectively, not recklessly. The rich often borrow against appreciating assets rather than selling them, preserving growth potential while accessing capital for new investments. For example, borrowing against a portfolio of stocks or real estate can fund business ventures or additional acquisitions without triggering taxes or reducing ownership. This disciplined use of leverage magnifies returns when managed carefully and supported by strong cash flow.

Liquidity holds a more strategic role than most people realize. While the wealthy often have significant sums invested in illiquid assets like private companies or real estate, they maintain accessible reserves to act quickly on emerging opportunities. This liquidity is not necessarily held as idle cash but may take the form of short-term bonds, cash-equivalent funds, or lines of credit secured against existing assets. The purpose is not safety for its own sake but the ability to move decisively when high-value opportunities appear, such as acquiring distressed properties during a downturn or investing in a promising startup before it scales.

Portfolio design also evolves with scale. At earlier stages, concentration can accelerate growth — focusing on a single business or market where one has expertise often produces the fastest wealth creation. As net worth grows, the focus shifts toward preservation and steady compounding. This is why ultra-wealthy individuals diversify broadly across industries and geographies, ensuring no single event can threaten their overall position. The transition from aggressive accumulation to careful preservation is gradual but deliberate, reflecting an understanding that strategies must shift as goals change.

Dynamic rebalancing plays a key role in sustaining performance. Rather than setting a portfolio and forgetting it, the wealthy reassess regularly to account for market conditions, new opportunities, and life changes. Rebalancing is not about chasing trends but about ensuring alignment with overarching objectives. If a single asset class has grown disproportionately, it may be trimmed to free capital for areas with higher potential or to restore the desired risk profile. This disciplined approach prevents emotional reactions during market swings and keeps decision-making grounded in strategy rather than impulse.

An often-overlooked factor is the integration of lifestyle with portfolio design. The rich do not separate their financial lives from their personal ambitions; they build portfolios that support the life they want to live. This can mean allocating funds toward philanthropic initiatives, impact investments, or legacy planning, ensuring wealth serves a purpose beyond accumulation. Portfolios become tools not just for personal security but for influence, contribution, and long-term family impact.

Risk management is woven into every layer of the structure. Insurance, legal protections, and thoughtful entity design shield wealth from unforeseen events. By compartmentalizing assets — for instance, holding real estate in separate entities or establishing trusts — they reduce exposure to liability while creating flexibility for future transfers. This level of foresight allows them to pursue ambitious strategies without jeopardizing the foundation they have built.

Why Liquidity and Timing Separate Winners from Losers

In wealth building, two factors quietly determine outcomes far more than raw intelligence or even access to opportunities: liquidity and timing. Liquidity is the ability to access capital without friction. Timing is the capacity to act decisively when conditions are optimal. Together, they dictate who seizes moments of transformation and who watches from the sidelines. Many people underestimate their significance, focusing solely on the quality of investments or the size of returns, while overlooking the practical ability to enter and exit at the right time.

The Power of Liquidity

Liquidity provides optionality. It allows you to respond rather than react. When markets shift or opportunities arise, those with liquid capital are positioned to take advantage while others remain trapped in illiquid commitments or scrambling to secure funds. This advantage compounds during crises, when prices drop and panic selling creates openings for disciplined buyers. Historically, many of the greatest fortunes were built by individuals and families who could deploy cash precisely when others could not.

This does not mean hoarding idle cash at all times. Liquidity can exist in various forms — cash reserves, short-term financial instruments, or even lines of credit secured by appreciating assets. The key is accessibility. If capital cannot be mobilized quickly, opportunities are missed. The wealthy often maintain layered liquidity, balancing immediate cash with assets that can be liquidated or borrowed against at favorable terms. This structure ensures they remain agile without sacrificing the growth potential of longer-term investments.

Timing as the Silent Multiplier

Equally critical is the art of timing. Buying into an opportunity too early can tie up resources unproductively; entering too late can mean competing at inflated prices or missing the window entirely. Timing requires both foresight and patience — the ability to prepare in advance, wait without anxiety, and act decisively when the moment arrives.

Market cycles illustrate this principle vividly. Those who bought real estate during downturns, when prices were depressed and sentiment was pessimistic, often saw exponential gains in the recovery. Similarly, early investors in transformative technologies — from the internet to renewable energy — reaped outsized rewards by recognizing shifts before they became mainstream. Yet in both cases, success depended not only on insight but on being prepared with capital and conviction at the critical moment.

The Intersection of Liquidity and Timing

Where liquidity and timing meet, opportunity accelerates. Having cash at the wrong time is nearly as limiting as having no cash at all. Likewise, recognizing an ideal moment without the resources to act breeds frustration rather than success. The winners are those who align both: they anticipate potential inflection points, preserve the capacity to act, and move decisively when conditions align with their strategy.

Building liquidity without sacrificing growth begins with intentional design. Instead of viewing cash as unproductive, treat it as strategic capital waiting for deployment. This mindset reframes reserves from a drag on returns to a source of future advantage. Allocating a portion of assets to highly liquid instruments such as short-term bonds, money market funds, or easily redeemable accounts provides flexibility while allowing modest growth. Beyond this, secured credit lines against appreciating assets — like real estate or investment portfolios — create additional layers of access without requiring liquidation. This layered approach ensures readiness without sidelining too much potential growth.

Preparation for timing windows requires both observation and patience. Opportunities rarely announce themselves in obvious ways. They appear quietly during moments of discomfort — when markets are volatile, when fear dominates headlines, or when industries are in transition. Training yourself to notice these inflection points involves studying broader trends, understanding market cycles, and keeping a clear perspective when others are distracted by short-term noise. Patience is equally vital; acting too early can lock up resources unnecessarily, while acting too late can erode the potential upside. The most effective investors learn to wait with readiness, holding capital steady until conditions align rather than forcing action out of restlessness.

Executing at the right moment demands clarity on your personal criteria for opportunity. Defining what constitutes a "yes" ahead of time prevents hesitation or second-guessing when the window opens. For some, this might mean a target price on an asset class, a set of conditions for entering a business venture, or a threshold of risk tolerance. These predetermined rules transform timing from guesswork into strategy, reducing emotional decision-making when the stakes are highest.

The discipline of aligning liquidity and timing also requires resisting social pressure. During market booms, holding cash or waiting on the sidelines can feel counterintuitive when others appear to be profiting. Yet the richest gains often come from acting against the crowd — buying when fear is rampant and selling or holding steady when euphoria peaks. This contrarian patience is not rooted in defiance but in preparation. It is the reward for having built liquidity and defined timing criteria long before conditions shift. Over time, this approach compounds advantages. Each well-timed move strengthens both capital and confidence, enabling larger and more decisive actions in the future. Missed opportunities, conversely, tend to reinforce hesitation, keeping individuals trapped in reactive cycles rather than proactive strategies. By mastering this interplay, you position yourself to benefit from both ordinary market cycles and rare moments of transformative change.

Chapter 8: The Psychology of Money Mastery

Behavioral Biases That Destroy Wealth

Wealth is often lost not because of a lack of opportunity or knowledge, but because of the way people think and behave under pressure. Even seasoned investors and entrepreneurs fall victim to mental shortcuts and emotional reactions that undermine rational decision-making. Understanding these biases is crucial for anyone who wants to protect and grow their wealth, because awareness alone can dramatically reduce their destructive influence.

Loss Aversion and the Fear of Losing

One of the most powerful psychological forces is loss aversion — the tendency to feel the pain of loss more intensely than the pleasure of gain. This bias makes individuals overly cautious when opportunities arise and overly emotional when investments decline. A person might hold onto underperforming assets far too long, hoping to "get back to even," or avoid promising opportunities entirely for fear of a temporary dip in value. The irony is that this bias, meant to protect from loss, often prevents the pursuit of gains that could far outweigh the risks.

Loss aversion also feeds into poor timing. Investors often sell at the bottom of market cycles, locking in losses, and then re-enter after prices have already recovered, missing the best returns. This reactive behavior not only erodes capital but reinforces anxiety, making it harder to commit to future strategies with confidence.

Confirmation Bias and the Echo Chamber Effect

Another common trap is confirmation bias — the tendency to seek out and trust information that supports existing beliefs while ignoring or dismissing evidence to the contrary. This bias creates a dangerous echo chamber where flawed assumptions go unchallenged.

For example, someone convinced that a particular investment will succeed may selectively focus on positive news about it while disregarding warning signs. Entrepreneurs are equally vulnerable, overlooking critical feedback about a business idea because it conflicts with their optimism. While confidence is essential for wealth creation, unchecked confirmation bias blinds decision-makers to real risks and prevents course corrections before problems escalate.

Overconfidence and the Illusion of Control

Overconfidence often appears after a period of success. When people experience a few wins — whether in the stock market, real estate, or business — they begin to believe they have superior insight or control over outcomes. This leads to taking outsized risks, overleveraging, or abandoning due diligence under the assumption that their intuition alone is sufficient.

The wealthy guard against overconfidence by implementing systems that check their decisions against objective criteria. They use advisors, written strategies, and structured reviews to keep ego from distorting judgment. Those who fail to establish these guardrails often discover too late that luck, not skill, fueled their earlier successes.

Herd Mentality and Social Pressure

Humans are social creatures, and this instinct can be costly when it comes to money. Herd mentality — the urge to follow the crowd — drives people to buy when everyone else is buying and sell when panic spreads. It is one of the primary reasons bubbles inflate and crashes deepen.

The pressure to conform is subtle but pervasive. Watching peers invest in trending assets or hearing stories of easy profits creates fear of missing out, leading individuals to abandon their own strategies in pursuit of quick gains. Yet history repeatedly shows that those who thrive long-term are often the ones willing to act contrary to the herd, maintaining discipline while others chase hype or flee in fear.

Anchoring bias exerts its influence when people fixate on an initial reference point — such as a purchase price, a past peak value, or an arbitrary benchmark — and use it to guide decisions even when circumstances change. This often leads to holding assets longer than appropriate or refusing opportunities that seem "too expensive" simply because they once cost less. Anchoring prevents objective assessment and can lock individuals into suboptimal strategies, especially in volatile markets where conditions evolve quickly.

Closely related is the sunk cost fallacy, where past investments of time, money, or effort distort future choices. Instead of objectively evaluating whether continuing is wise, people persist because they feel committed to what they have already put in. Entrepreneurs keep funding failing ventures, investors double down on losing positions, and professionals stay in unfulfilling careers because of years already spent. In reality, past costs are unrecoverable; rational decisions should focus on future potential rather than emotional attachment to what has already been lost.

Recency bias further compounds poor decision-making by placing undue weight on recent experiences. A string of positive returns may lead to complacency, convincing someone that current conditions will last indefinitely. Conversely, a period of losses can cause excessive pessimism, prompting premature withdrawal from opportunities that remain fundamentally sound. Both extremes distort long-term strategy, as short-term emotions override objective analysis of broader trends.

Another subtle but damaging bias is the availability heuristic — the tendency to overestimate the likelihood of events that are easiest to recall. Dramatic stories of sudden wealth or catastrophic loss, amplified by media, often skew perception of risk and reward. People avoid sound investments because of memorable market crashes or chase speculative opportunities after hearing sensational success stories. This mental shortcut fuels overreaction, swinging decision-making between extremes of fear and greed rather than grounded evaluation.

Mitigating these biases begins with building deliberate systems. Written investment principles, automatic rebalancing, and predefined exit criteria reduce impulsive decisions in moments of stress. Seeking external perspectives, whether from mentors, advisors, or peers, provides a reality check against personal blind spots. Reviewing decisions after the fact — not just outcomes, but the reasoning behind them — strengthens awareness and improves future judgment.

Cultivating emotional discipline is equally vital. Practices like pausing before major financial moves, grounding decisions in data rather than headlines, and reframing setbacks as learning opportunities help neutralize reactive tendencies. Awareness of these biases does not eliminate them but creates the space to respond thoughtfully rather than impulsively.

Delayed Gratification vs. Accelerated Growth

The tension between delayed gratification and accelerated growth is one of the most defining dynamics in wealth building. Traditional financial wisdom glorifies patience — save diligently, invest steadily, and wait decades for compound interest to work its magic. In contrast, entrepreneurial paths often emphasize speed — leverage skills, seize opportunities, and scale rapidly to achieve financial independence far sooner. Both approaches have merit, but understanding how and when to apply them is critical to avoiding extremes that either stunt potential or create unnecessary risk.

The Psychology of Delayed Gratification

Delayed gratification is rooted in the ability to forgo immediate pleasure for long-term reward. The famous "marshmallow test" demonstrated how children willing to wait for a bigger payoff later tended to achieve greater success as adults. In personal finance, this principle translates into saving consistently, resisting lifestyle inflation, and reinvesting gains rather than spending them prematurely.

The power of delayed gratification lies in compounding. A modest investment, left untouched, can grow exponentially over decades. This is the cornerstone of retirement planning and the reason time in the market is often more powerful than timing the market. It fosters discipline and creates a buffer against impulsive decisions that derail financial goals.

However, strict adherence to delayed gratification has its drawbacks. Waiting too long to enjoy the fruits of your labor can lead to missed experiences and opportunities for growth. It can also create a mindset of perpetual postponement, where life is always about future goals rather than present fulfillment. In extreme cases, people become so focused on saving that they underinvest in themselves — neglecting education, relationships, or ventures that could multiply their income and accelerate their timeline.

The Case for Accelerated Growth

Accelerated growth focuses on compressing timelines by pursuing opportunities with higher leverage. Rather than waiting decades for gradual accumulation, this approach seeks exponential gains through entrepreneurship, strategic risk-taking, or acquiring equity in high-potential ventures. It aligns with the mindset of building once and earning repeatedly, using systems and assets that continue producing value beyond personal effort.

This path appeals to those unwilling to settle for incremental progress. It recognizes that certain opportunities — technological innovations, market shifts, or emerging trends — reward speed and boldness. Acting decisively during these windows can generate outcomes unattainable through traditional saving alone. Many self-made millionaires credit their success not to frugality but to seizing these pivotal moments and scaling aggressively while conditions favored rapid expansion.

Yet accelerated growth carries inherent risks. High-reward opportunities often involve uncertainty, and missteps can lead to significant losses if not carefully managed. Without proper preparation — financial cushions, adaptable strategies, and emotional resilience — the pursuit of speed can backfire, leaving individuals worse off than if they had followed a slower, steadier path.

The most effective wealth builders understand that these two approaches are not mutually exclusive but complementary. They save and reinvest to create stability, while selectively pursuing high-growth opportunities that can compress timelines. The challenge lies in knowing when to prioritize patience and when to lean into decisive action — a balance that shifts with life stage, market conditions, and personal goals.

Blending the two approaches begins with identifying a financial foundation that supports calculated risk-taking. A stable base of savings, income, and low personal expenses provides the security necessary to pursue higher-growth ventures without jeopardizing basic needs. This foundation acts as a safety net, reducing the fear-driven decision-making that often leads to abandoning opportunities prematurely or overcommitting to unsafe levels of risk.

Once stability is in place, the next step is selective acceleration. Not every opportunity warrants aggressive pursuit. Filtering for asymmetric upside — situations where potential gains far outweigh the downside — ensures that energy and capital are concentrated on plays that truly justify the shift from patience to speed. This selectivity prevents the common pitfall of chasing every trend or forcing growth in unsuitable conditions, both of which erode long-term momentum.

Timing is critical in executing this balance. Market cycles and personal readiness rarely align perfectly, but those who prepare in advance position themselves to act when windows of opportunity open. Building skills, relationships, and liquidity ahead of time allows decisive action when conditions turn favorable. This preparation also minimizes regret, as decisions are grounded in readiness rather than impulsive reaction to external hype or pressure.

Psychological flexibility plays a central role in sustaining this dual strategy. People who overly identify with one approach often resist switching gears even when circumstances demand it. A long-term saver may hesitate to seize transformative opportunities, while an aggressive growth seeker may struggle to downshift into preservation once success is achieved. Developing the ability to transition between patience and boldness — without guilt, fear, or ego — is what separates those who adapt and thrive from those who stagnate in one mode.

An overlooked but vital aspect of this dynamic is reinvestment. Gains from accelerated growth should not fuel lifestyle inflation but rather feed back into the foundation that supports future moves. This creates a cycle where each successful leap increases stability, which in turn enables even bolder and better-calculated opportunities. Over time, this compounding effect blends the strengths of both strategies: the exponential upside of growth paired with the enduring resilience of delayed gratification.

The deeper reward of mastering this balance is not purely financial. It is the freedom to choose your pace at every stage of life. When to slow down and savor, when to sprint and stretch, when to preserve and when to multiply. This adaptability ensures wealth serves as a tool for building a meaningful life rather than a goal pursued for its own sake. The ability to navigate between patience and acceleration with clarity and intention transforms wealth building from a rigid formula into an evolving art — one that grows alongside you, shaped by both vision and timing rather than fear or default habit.

The Quiet Discipline of the Ultra-Wealthy

To an outside observer, the lives of the ultra-wealthy may seem defined by privilege, luxury, and indulgence. Yet beneath the surface lies a quality far less visible but far more critical to their enduring success: quiet discipline. This discipline is not loud, performative, or even easily understood by those who equate wealth with constant spending. It is the steady commitment to habits and decisions that prioritize preservation and growth over the fleeting thrill of display.

Beyond Flash and Performance

Popular culture often glamorizes wealth as something to flaunt — cars, watches, lavish homes. While some individuals do fall into that pattern, many of the world's enduringly wealthy live with a restraint that surprises outsiders. They do not measure their success by what they can show but by the freedom and security they quietly accumulate. This mindset shift creates an entirely different relationship with money. Wealth becomes a tool rather than a trophy, allowing choices based on vision and values rather than social validation.

This is why, in many cases, the ultra-wealthy appear understated. Their homes may be comfortable but not ostentatious. Their clothes practical rather than loud. Their financial decisions prioritize long-term resilience rather than short-term optics. This restraint is not rooted in frugality for its own sake but in an understanding that reputation and sustainability matter far more than temporary admiration.

The Power of Consistency

The discipline of the ultra-wealthy is built on consistency rather than occasional bursts of effort. Small decisions, repeated over years, create the foundation for fortunes that last generations. This shows up in meticulous attention to budgets, regular reviews of investments, and a deliberate pace in scaling ventures. While outsiders may focus on singular "big wins," insiders know it is the steady accumulation of disciplined choices that compounds into extraordinary results.

Consistency also extends to personal development. Many ultra-wealthy individuals maintain daily routines that prioritize health, learning, and focus.

They guard their time carefully, understanding that energy and clarity are as valuable as capital. Morning routines, exercise habits, and intentional reflection are not luxuries; they are non-negotiables that support high-level decision-making and sustained performance.

Emotional Control and Patience

Quiet discipline is as much about managing emotions as managing money. The ultra-wealthy learn to detach from the highs and lows of markets, opportunities, and public opinion. They do not chase trends or panic during downturns. Instead, they cultivate patience — waiting for the right openings, holding positions through volatility, and resisting the urge to react impulsively to temporary noise.

This patience is what enables them to play the long game. They understand that wealth is not built or destroyed in a single transaction but shaped over decades. By staying grounded, they position themselves to benefit from compounding forces that elude those who seek instant results.

This discipline shows up most clearly in how decisions are made. Choices are filtered through long-term impact rather than immediate gratification. Before committing capital, they ask how it aligns with their vision, what risks it introduces, and how it contributes to stability. This clarity of intention keeps them from overextending during booms or retreating in fear during downturns. Their wealth grows not because they avoid mistakes entirely, but because they minimize avoidable errors and recover quickly from the inevitable ones.

Behind this decision-making is a commitment to structure. The ultra-wealthy do not rely on memory or intuition alone; they build systems that guide behavior. These systems include scheduled portfolio reviews, automatic reinvestment strategies, and clearly defined criteria for when to buy, hold, or exit investments. Such frameworks reduce emotional interference and maintain discipline even under pressure. They also extend beyond finances into lifestyle — boundaries around work, rest, and personal commitments ensure sustained performance and prevent burnout that can derail even the best strategies.

An equally important element is discretion. Quiet discipline means avoiding unnecessary exposure and resisting the impulse to broadcast every success. Privacy protects not only personal safety but also decision-making clarity.

When public opinion does not drive choices, it is easier to maintain focus on genuine goals rather than perform for approval. This discretion allows flexibility to pivot, experiment, or even fail without the weight of external judgment.

Another subtle expression of discipline is continuous learning. The ultra-wealthy remain students of markets, industries, and themselves. They read extensively, seek counsel from mentors, and pay attention to shifts in culture and technology. This ongoing curiosity prevents complacency, ensuring they remain prepared for emerging opportunities and evolving risks. Their learning is rarely reactive; it is built into their lifestyle as a quiet but deliberate habit.

The impact of these practices is cumulative. Individually, no single habit seems extraordinary — a regular review here, a morning routine there, a cautious investment decision once in a while. But repeated consistently over years, these small acts form the backbone of lasting wealth. They shield fortunes from erosion, position individuals to capitalize on rare moments of advantage, and ensure that success endures beyond one generation.

This level of discipline is available to anyone willing to cultivate it. It does not require vast resources to begin. It begins with small commitments to structure and patience: tracking spending, defining personal values, building emergency reserves, or simply pausing before major financial decisions. Over time, these small disciplines create the same foundation the ultra-wealthy rely on — the quiet, almost invisible strength that allows them to remain steady regardless of circumstance.

Part IV. The Hidden Game of Legacy and Meaning

There comes a point in the pursuit of wealth where the questions change. It is no longer about how to earn more, protect more, or multiply more. The focus shifts to why — why pursue wealth at all, and what should it ultimately serve? For many, this realization arrives quietly, often after they have achieved financial security and discover that freedom alone is not enough. The deeper pursuit begins: creating something that lasts, something that matters beyond their own lifetime.

Legacy is rarely about monuments or public recognition. It is about the invisible impact of choices carried forward — the opportunities created for future generations, the values instilled in family and community, the contributions made to causes that outlive personal ambition. The ultra-wealthy understand this hidden game because they have seen firsthand that financial success without meaning feels hollow. True wealth is measured not just by numbers on a balance sheet, but by the lives touched and the ripple effects set in motion long after one's presence is gone.

This part of the book explores the quiet but profound shift from accumulation to stewardship. It looks at how wealth can become a vehicle for impact rather than simply consumption, and how intentional design — in family, business, and philanthropy — creates continuity where others experience fragmentation. It also confronts the challenges of legacy: maintaining unity across generations, balancing freedom with responsibility, and ensuring that wealth enhances rather than erodes character.

The hidden game is not about perfection but alignment. It asks you to define what matters most and to design your financial life to reflect those priorities. This is where wealth transcends survival and success to become a source of meaning — a foundation not just for personal freedom, but for lasting contribution.

Chapter 9: Hidden Networks and Gatekeepers

Finding and Entering Wealth Circles

For anyone seeking to accelerate their financial journey, the people they surround themselves with often matter as much as the strategies they pursue. Wealth circles — the networks of individuals who operate at higher levels of knowledge, opportunity, and influence — shape how information flows, where deals are made, and what doors open. Yet these circles are rarely advertised, and entry is seldom achieved through force or superficial tactics. It requires intentional positioning, value creation, and a shift in how you view relationships.

Why Wealth Circles Matter

The wealthy operate in environments where opportunities are shared quietly. The most profitable investments, the most transformative partnerships, and even the most valuable insights often never appear on public platforms. They move through trusted networks, where reputation and alignment matter more than formal applications or credentials. Being in the right rooms exposes you to different ways of thinking — not just financial strategies but the mindset, patience, and long-term vision that underpin enduring wealth.

This access creates a compounding effect. A single introduction can lead to a cascade of partnerships, mentorships, and opportunities that transform the trajectory of your financial life. But it is not only about what you gain. These circles also challenge you to raise your standards. The expectations, conversations, and behaviors in these environments subtly reshape what you consider normal. Over time, this shift in reference points can be as valuable as the opportunities themselves.

Preparing Yourself Before Entering

Many underestimate the preparation required before seeking entry into wealth circles. These networks are built on trust, and trust is extended only when you demonstrate reliability, discretion, and mutual value. Before approaching these environments, it is worth asking: what do I bring? Skills, insights, connections, or even simply a grounded perspective can all be valuable — but they must be authentic. People can sense opportunism, and nothing closes doors faster than the perception of taking without contributing.

Equally important is alignment of mindset. Wealth circles are not simply about ambition; they are about stewardship and vision. Individuals at this level think in terms of decades, not days. They focus on building systems rather than chasing trends. If you enter with a short-term, transactional approach, you will stand out for the wrong reasons. Shifting your own perspective to prioritize growth, contribution, and long-term thinking makes you more magnetic to those already living that reality.

Finding Where the Circles Exist

These circles do not always gather where you might expect. While luxury events and high-profile conferences can provide entry points, many of the most valuable relationships form in more subtle spaces — industry-specific masterminds, private investor groups, philanthropic boards, or even niche communities centered around shared passions. In recent years, online platforms have also opened doors to curated groups that would have once been geographically out of reach.

Identifying these spaces requires research and discernment. Look for environments where value is exchanged rather than flaunted, where learning and collaboration outweigh performance. A room full of people broadcasting their success is rarely where enduring opportunities are forged. Instead, seek rooms where the conversations challenge you to think bigger, refine your strategies, and connect authentically.

Positioning yourself begins with presence rather than persuasion. In high-trust environments, people notice consistency more than self-promotion. Showing up repeatedly, contributing to discussions, and offering help without expecting immediate return builds familiarity. Over time, this quiet consistency becomes the basis for deeper conversations and opportunities that would never arise from a single impressive pitch.

Credibility is built through action rather than claims. Sharing practical insights from your own experiences, introducing people who might benefit from knowing one another, or delivering on small commitments demonstrates reliability. These seemingly minor actions establish a reputation as someone who adds value, which in turn invites reciprocity. In circles where reputation spreads quickly, this form of quiet credibility becomes one of the most powerful currencies you can hold.

Another aspect of positioning is humility paired with curiosity. Entering a wealth circle with the attitude of a learner opens far more doors than posturing as an expert. Asking thoughtful questions, listening deeply, and being willing to absorb perspectives different from your own signals respect. This curiosity fosters genuine connection, because people sense that you value their insights rather than viewing them solely as means to an end.

Building authentic relationships requires patience. The most impactful connections are rarely formed through transactional networking but through shared experiences and mutual trust developed over time. This might happen through collaboration on projects, participating in small group discussions, or simply maintaining consistent contact outside formal events. Approaching these relationships with the mindset of contribution rather than extraction ensures they deepen naturally and endure far longer.

As you integrate into these circles, discretion becomes crucial. The wealthy value privacy, and respect for confidentiality separates those who are welcomed from those who are quietly excluded. Avoiding unnecessary name-dropping, handling sensitive information with care, and focusing on building trust rather than showcasing access are non-negotiable. This respect for privacy not only protects relationships but also positions you as someone safe to involve in future opportunities.

Over time, participation in these circles shifts your own perspective. The conversations challenge assumptions about what is possible, encourage bolder thinking, and reveal strategies unavailable in mainstream environments. Observing how others navigate setbacks, manage risk, and align wealth with purpose provides models that accelerate your own growth. Perhaps most importantly, these circles normalize ambition and long-term vision, replacing any lingering doubts about whether extraordinary outcomes are realistic for you.

The Currency of Trust and Reputation

In the world of wealth creation and high-level opportunity, trust and reputation function as forms of currency more valuable than money itself. While capital can be replenished, trust takes years to build and moments to lose. Reputation, shaped by consistent behavior and perceptions over time, determines the quality of opportunities available, the depth of partnerships formed, and the extent to which others are willing to support or collaborate with you. Understanding and cultivating this currency is essential for anyone aiming to move beyond transactional relationships and into the realm of enduring influence and access.

Why Trust Matters More Than Transactions

Trust transforms financial and business interactions from mere exchanges into collaborative endeavors. When trust is present, agreements can be more flexible, negotiations more straightforward, and risks more manageable. Investors back ventures because they believe in the people, not just the numbers. Partners commit to joint projects because they are confident in each other's integrity and competence. In wealth circles, where deals often lack formal contracts or are structured informally, trust becomes the binding force that ensures commitments are honored.

This reliance on trust also accelerates opportunities. People are more likely to introduce trusted individuals to their own networks, share exclusive information, and support ventures beyond what is strictly required. Trust creates a multiplier effect, where one positive reputation can open doors to a web of possibilities that would remain closed otherwise.

Reputation as a Reflection of Character and Competence

Reputation is the cumulative result of how you show up consistently in the eyes of others. It blends character — honesty, reliability, and respect — with competence — skill, knowledge, and results. In environments where wealth and influence are concentrated, reputation spreads quickly, often preceding direct interaction. This means your name carries a story, shaped by every interaction, decision, and communication, whether intentional or not.

Maintaining a strong reputation requires vigilance. Even small lapses in judgment or integrity can damage trust and, by extension, your ability to access future opportunities. Conversely, acts of generosity, transparency, and follow-through reinforce positive perceptions, creating a reservoir of goodwill that can sustain you through challenges.

The Role of Consistency and Transparency

Consistency is the foundation of reputation. It means delivering on promises repeatedly, communicating openly, and behaving predictably in ways that reinforce trust. People feel secure when they can anticipate your responses and rely on your commitments. Transparency further enhances this by reducing uncertainty. While full disclosure is neither possible nor advisable in every situation, sharing relevant information honestly and proactively builds confidence and reduces the potential for misunderstandings.

Recovering trust when mistakes occur is as important as building it initially. The ultra-wealthy understand that errors are inevitable in complex ventures but also recognize that damage to reputation can be minimized through accountability and clear communication. Owning up to mistakes promptly, outlining corrective actions, and following through transparently rebuilds confidence. This approach not only preserves relationships but often deepens respect, as it demonstrates integrity and commitment to continuous improvement rather than perfectionism.

Communication is a vital tool in managing trust and reputation. Clarity in conveying intentions, expectations, and limitations prevents misunderstandings that can erode goodwill. Active listening plays a complementary role by ensuring that others feel heard and understood, strengthening relational bonds. In high-stakes environments, subtle cues such as tone, timing, and empathy can be as impactful as the content of the message itself. Mastering these interpersonal dynamics is essential for sustaining the currency of trust over time.

Boundaries also play a crucial role. Trust does not mean unlimited availability or unquestioning agreement. Healthy boundaries communicate self-respect and set clear parameters for interaction. They protect your time, energy, and focus, ensuring that relationships are sustainable and mutually beneficial. By establishing what you will and will not tolerate, you create a framework that encourages accountability from both sides and prevents exploitation or burnout.

Building trust and reputation is a long-term endeavor that requires patience and intentionality. It is not built through quick wins or superficial charm but through repeated acts of integrity, competence, and respect. The process involves continuously aligning words with actions, following through on commitments, and treating every interaction as an opportunity to reinforce your personal brand.

Information Arbitrage: Profiting from What Others Don't See

One of the quietest but most powerful forces behind wealth creation is the ability to spot opportunities before they become obvious. Information arbitrage involves leveraging insights, data, or perspectives that are available to you but not yet recognized or acted upon by others. It is the practice of identifying discrepancies in knowledge and using them to gain a strategic advantage. This skill separates those who merely participate in markets from those who shape them.

The Nature of Information Arbitrage

Information is rarely evenly distributed. Whether due to geography, networks, expertise, or access, some individuals see patterns and possibilities others miss. This creates an imbalance that can be exploited for financial gain. Unlike traditional arbitrage, which deals with price differences across markets, information arbitrage focuses on knowledge gaps and timing advantages.

This practice is not about insider trading or unethical conduct but about developing unique angles through diligent research, experience, and perspective. For example, a real estate investor who notices early signs of neighborhood revitalization can purchase properties before prices rise. An entrepreneur aware of emerging regulatory changes might create solutions before competitors respond. In each case, the arbitrage exists because the information is not yet widespread or interpreted fully by the market.

Sources of Information Advantage

The sources of informational advantage are diverse. Professional networks provide early warnings about industry shifts or investment opportunities. Niche communities and specialized forums offer deep insights that mainstream media overlook. Continuous learning through books, courses, and mentorship sharpens the ability to synthesize data into actionable foresight.

Technology also plays a role, enabling faster analysis of trends, access to data, and communication with experts worldwide. Yet technology alone is insufficient without critical thinking. The true arbitrage lies in combining raw information with context and judgment to see what others do not.

Developing an Arbitrage Mindset

Cultivating the mindset necessary for information arbitrage requires curiosity, skepticism, and patience. Curiosity drives the quest for knowledge beyond surface-level headlines. Skepticism prevents acceptance of conventional wisdom without scrutiny. Patience allows time for insights to mature and markets to respond. Together, these traits encourage deeper engagement with the environment and reduce the risk of jumping prematurely on untested ideas.

A key skill in this process is pattern recognition — connecting seemingly unrelated dots to reveal emerging trends or hidden opportunities. This ability is developed through diverse experiences, interdisciplinary study, and deliberate reflection. By broadening your mental models, you increase the likelihood of identifying gaps in others' understanding.

Successful implementation of information arbitrage depends on building tailored networks that expose you to unique insights. This means cultivating relationships with experts, insiders, and thought leaders who operate in niches aligned with your goals. These connections often provide early warnings or perspectives unavailable to the general public. Maintaining these networks requires genuine engagement, offering value in return rather than transactional requests. Over time, trust builds and access deepens, creating a flow of information that is both timely and relevant.

Filtering signal from noise is essential. The modern information environment is flooded with data, opinions, and speculation, making it challenging to discern what truly matters. Developing criteria for evaluating sources, cross-referencing facts, and focusing on actionable intelligence allows you to avoid distraction and focus your energy on insights that can move the needle. This discipline sharpens decision-making and prevents costly mistakes born from reacting to incomplete or misleading information.

Converting insights into concrete action is the final and most critical step. Information arbitrage is useless without execution. This means designing systems that translate knowledge into investments, partnerships, or innovations efficiently. It also requires a bias toward experimentation —

testing hypotheses on a small scale, learning from outcomes, and scaling successful initiatives. Through this iterative process, you refine your ability to capitalize on emerging trends before they become obvious to others.

Patience and timing remain vital throughout. Even the most compelling insights can take time to materialize into value. The arbitrage opportunity exists in the gap between discovery and market recognition. Maintaining readiness to act when that gap closes involves liquidity, flexibility, and emotional discipline — qualities that support seizing advantage without undue haste or fear.

Chapter 10: Crisis, Chaos, and Opportunity

How the Elite Profit During Downturns

Economic downturns and market crashes inspire fear and uncertainty for most people. The instinctive reaction is often to retreat, protect assets, or abandon investments to preserve capital. While this fear is understandable, it also creates a distinct divide between those who lose ground and those who emerge stronger. The elite profit during downturns not by ignoring risks but by understanding and leveraging them strategically. They recognize that these challenging periods are not just obstacles but unique opportunities to acquire value and accelerate wealth building.

The Mindset of Opportunity

The first distinguishing trait is mindset. Rather than viewing downturns as catastrophic events, the elite see them as moments of transformation. Market corrections expose inefficiencies and reset valuations, creating openings that are unavailable during times of exuberance. This mindset is rooted in long-term thinking and emotional discipline — the ability to detach from panic and focus on the underlying fundamentals of assets and businesses.

Viewing downturns as opportunity rather than threat allows the elite to act decisively when others hesitate. While most are frozen by fear or overwhelmed by negative news, the elite are calmly evaluating what assets have become undervalued and which strategies position them best for the recovery. This perspective shifts their behavior from reactive to proactive, enabling them to move first and secure advantages that compound over time.

Building Liquidity in Preparation

One of the practical steps the elite take long before downturns occur is maintaining liquidity. Having readily accessible capital — whether in cash reserves, liquid investments, or credit lines — provides the ability to purchase assets at discounted prices without needing to sell other holdings prematurely. This preparation prevents them from being forced into selling at losses or missing opportunities due to lack of funds.

Liquidity also affords flexibility. During volatile times, the elite can diversify or concentrate their investments based on emerging trends rather than being constrained by cash flow. This agility is crucial for capitalizing on fast-moving situations that require quick decisions and execution.

Deep Research and Due Diligence

The elite deepen their research during downturns, using the pause in market activity to identify undervalued assets with strong fundamentals. They analyze balance sheets, management teams, market positioning, and industry dynamics with greater scrutiny. This thorough due diligence allows them to distinguish between temporary market noise and structural weaknesses, enabling them to make informed investments with higher confidence.

Unlike the average investor who may be swayed by headlines or short-term volatility, the elite rely on disciplined frameworks and trusted advisors to guide their decisions. This approach minimizes emotional errors and focuses capital where it has the highest probability of recovery and growth. During downturns, the elite often turn to acquiring distressed assets — businesses, properties, or investments that others avoid due to perceived risk or liquidity issues. These assets are frequently priced below intrinsic value because the market sentiment is dominated by fear and uncertainty. The elite approach these opportunities with a strategic mindset, assessing whether the challenges are temporary and can be resolved through operational improvements, restructuring, or market recovery. By purchasing at significant discounts, they set the stage for outsized returns as conditions normalize.

Counter-cyclical investments form another pillar of their strategy. While most investors retreat from sectors hit hardest by economic contractions, the elite look for industries that historically rebound stronger or benefit from shifts in consumer behavior during downturns. For example, discount retailers, repair services, or essential goods producers may see increased demand even in challenging times. Investing in these areas requires careful analysis but can provide steady income and capital appreciation while broader markets languish.

Leverage is used judiciously to amplify returns without compromising stability. Borrowing against existing assets at favorable rates allows the elite to increase their purchasing power precisely when asset prices are depressed. This use of debt is backed by conservative risk management and contingency planning to avoid forced sales if conditions worsen. The key difference is discipline — while many increase leverage during boom times, the elite often reserve this strategy for downturns when their ability to service debt is more secure relative to asset prices.

Active management distinguishes their approach further. Rather than passively holding investments, the elite engage deeply with acquired assets, deploying expertise and resources to enhance value. This might involve restructuring operations, upgrading management, or pivoting business models. Such hands-on involvement accelerates recovery and growth, transforming distressed purchases into competitive advantages.

Timing the exit is equally important. The elite prepare exit strategies that align with market cycles and valuation inflection points. They avoid the temptation to sell too early for modest gains or hold too long and risk reversal. By maintaining flexibility and monitoring macroeconomic signals, they optimize returns and recycle capital efficiently.

Beyond financial returns, downturns provide intangible benefits. They offer lessons in risk management, patience, and adaptability that strengthen decision-making for future cycles. They also build credibility and relationships, as those who act wisely during crises gain respect and attract collaborators who value steady leadership.

The Hidden Patterns of Economic Cycles

Economic cycles shape the landscape of wealth creation in ways both subtle and profound. While markets often seem chaotic and unpredictable, beneath the surface lie recurring patterns that govern expansion, contraction, and recovery. Recognizing these hidden rhythms is essential for aligning financial strategies with the broader forces at play, enabling more informed decisions that ride waves rather than fight them.

Understanding the Basics of Cycles

Economic cycles consist of phases: expansion, peak, contraction, and trough. During expansion, economic activity grows, employment rises, and asset prices generally increase. This phase is marked by optimism and investment. The peak represents the turning point where growth slows and imbalances begin to surface. Contraction follows, characterized by declining output, rising unemployment, and falling asset values. The trough marks the lowest point, setting the stage for recovery and a new expansion.

These phases repeat over time, but their duration and intensity vary depending on underlying factors such as technological innovation, monetary policy, geopolitical events, and consumer behavior. While no two cycles are identical, the patterns of human psychology — fear, greed, optimism, and panic — create consistent dynamics that influence market movements and economic activity.

The Role of Human Behavior

At the heart of economic cycles is the collective behavior of millions of individuals and institutions. During expansions, confidence fuels spending and investment, often pushing valuations beyond sustainable levels. This exuberance can mask underlying risks and lead to speculative bubbles. When reality sets in, fear takes hold, triggering sell-offs, credit tightening, and reduced consumption.

Understanding these emotional drivers helps explain why cycles are not purely mechanical but intertwined with sentiment. Recognizing when optimism turns to complacency or when fear shifts to opportunity provides an edge in navigating the phases with greater clarity.

Identifying Leading and Lagging Indicators

Effective interpretation of economic cycles involves tracking various indicators. Leading indicators, such as new orders in manufacturing, building permits, or stock market trends, provide early signals about the direction of the economy. Lagging indicators, like unemployment rates and corporate earnings, confirm trends but change after the broader shifts have begun.

By analyzing a combination of these metrics, seasoned investors and strategists anticipate turning points before they become evident to the wider public. This foresight allows positioning portfolios, adjusting risk, and capitalizing on emerging phases rather than reacting after the fact.

Over the past century, historical cycles have revealed variations in length and intensity influenced by technological breakthroughs and policy responses. The Industrial Revolution introduced prolonged expansions as productivity surged. More recently, globalization and digital innovation have accelerated information flows and market reactions, compressing some cycles while amplifying volatility. Central bank policies, such as interest rate adjustments and quantitative easing, now play a more direct role in moderating or extending phases of expansion and contraction.

Understanding these evolving factors allows investors to adjust expectations and strategies. For example, the rapid dissemination of information today means markets can price in expectations faster, reducing the lag between emerging trends and market response. This demands greater agility and a nuanced reading of indicators beyond traditional measures.

Practically applying knowledge of economic cycles involves balancing caution with opportunity. During expansion phases, it is tempting to maximize exposure to growth assets, but seasoned investors also begin positioning for eventual contraction by increasing diversification and liquidity. Conversely, contractions signal the importance of seeking undervalued assets and preparing for recovery, while managing risk through hedging or defensive positions.

Long-term wealth builders recognize that timing the market perfectly is impossible. Instead, they focus on aligning their portfolios with the cycle's broader trajectory, adjusting gradually rather than reacting impulsively. This approach smooths returns and reduces emotional stress, allowing them to capitalize on both bull and bear phases.

Another valuable strategy is studying sector rotation patterns. Different industries lead or lag at various points in the cycle. For example, consumer staples and utilities often outperform during contractions due to consistent demand, while technology and discretionary sectors thrive in expansions. Shifting allocation in response to these patterns enhances portfolio resilience and growth potential.

Finally, integrating economic cycle awareness with behavioral discipline enhances decision-making. Recognizing the psychological phases of the cycle — from fear to greed — helps investors check biases and maintain objectivity. This combination of technical insight and emotional intelligence creates a foundation for enduring financial success.

By decoding the hidden patterns of economic cycles, you gain a powerful framework to anticipate change, manage risk, and seize opportunities. This knowledge transforms uncertainty from an obstacle into a strategic advantage, enabling you to build wealth that not only grows but endures through the inevitable ups and downs of markets and economies.

Building Antifragile Wealth

In the pursuit of lasting wealth, resilience is often considered the ultimate goal. The ability to withstand shocks, downturns, and unforeseen challenges defines many successful financial journeys. Yet there is a deeper concept that transcends mere resilience: antifragility. Coined by philosopher Nassim Nicholas Taleb, antifragility describes systems that do more than survive stress — they improve and grow stronger because of it. Applying this principle to wealth creation transforms how you think about risk, opportunity, and long-term growth.

The Difference Between Resilience and Antifragility

Resilience is the capacity to endure shocks without breaking. A resilient portfolio weathers market declines without catastrophic loss, while a resilient business adapts to changing conditions and avoids collapse. Antifragility, however, takes this further. An antifragile system gains from disorder, volatility, and stressors. It uses challenges as inputs for evolution, learning, and expansion.

For wealth, this means building structures and strategies that capitalize on uncertainty rather than merely avoiding it. Rather than seeking a stable, predictable path that limits downside, antifragile wealth embraces variability, positioning to benefit when the unexpected occurs. This approach acknowledges that risk is inevitable but transforms it into an advantage rather than a threat.

Characteristics of Antifragile Wealth

Antifragile wealth is diversified not only across asset classes but also across sources of return and time horizons. It balances stable income streams with high-leverage opportunities that may be volatile but offer exponential upside. This creates a dynamic system where losses in one area can be offset or even turned into gains elsewhere.

Another key feature is redundancy. Like a well-designed safety net, antifragile wealth includes buffers and backups that prevent collapse. These may take the form of liquidity reserves, conservative holdings, or alternative investments that perform well under different scenarios. Redundancy does not mean inefficiency; rather, it provides optionality and flexibility when conditions shift.

The mindset behind antifragile wealth is one of experimentation and iterative improvement. Rather than rigidly adhering to a fixed plan, the antifragile investor tests ideas on small scales, learns from outcomes, and adapts. This reduces exposure to catastrophic failure while capturing gains from successful innovations or shifts.

Building antifragile wealth requires deliberate portfolio construction that blends stability with optionality. Stable income sources such as dividend-paying stocks, rental properties, or bonds provide a foundation that withstands normal fluctuations. Layered onto this foundation are higher-risk, higher-reward positions like startups, venture funds, or commodities, which may be volatile but offer the chance for outsized gains. This combination ensures that when volatility strikes, gains in some areas can absorb losses in others and even create new opportunities for growth.

Incorporating alternative investments enhances antifragility by reducing correlation with traditional markets. Assets such as private equity, real assets, or niche collectibles respond differently to economic forces, creating natural hedges. These alternatives often require deeper expertise and due diligence but reward those who can identify unique value.

Redundancy is also expressed through liquidity management. Holding accessible capital allows you to act quickly when market dislocations reveal bargains. This readiness to deploy cash or credit lines transforms uncertainty into advantage rather than constraint. Overleveraging during calm periods is avoided; instead, debt is used strategically when conditions favor entry at discounted prices.

Cultivating an antifragile mindset is as important as structural design. Embracing uncertainty means accepting that not all experiments will succeed, but each provides learning that strengthens future decisions. Patience and emotional discipline are required to avoid overreacting to short-term setbacks, instead viewing them as integral to growth. This mindset encourages adaptability — shifting tactics as new information emerges rather than clinging rigidly to outdated plans.

Practical habits include regular portfolio reviews that assess whether allocations maintain the balance of stability and optionality. Adjustments may involve trimming positions that have become overly concentrated or adding new opportunities aligned with emerging trends. Maintaining this dynamic balance is a continuous process, reflecting the evolving nature of markets and personal goals.

Additionally, building antifragile wealth involves protecting capital through legal and structural means. Asset protection strategies such as trusts, holding companies, and diversified legal entities create barriers against unexpected liabilities or economic shocks. These structures preserve wealth across generations and provide the flexibility to adapt ownership or control without disrupting underlying assets.

Chapter 11: The Generational Game

Building Wealth That Outlives You

The pursuit of wealth is often framed as a personal journey — accumulating assets, securing financial freedom, and enjoying the rewards of hard work. Yet for many who reach significant levels of success, the focus inevitably expands beyond individual gain toward something far more enduring: building wealth that outlives you. This shift in perspective moves from accumulation to stewardship, from self-interest to legacy, and requires new strategies, mindsets, and commitments that ensure the fruits of your labor continue to serve future generations and causes you care about.

The Meaning of Lasting Wealth

Lasting wealth is not simply about passing on money. It is about creating structures that preserve, grow, and responsibly distribute assets while reflecting your values. It encompasses financial security for heirs, the funding of philanthropic efforts, and the fostering of principles that sustain wealth beyond mere dollars. Wealth that outlives you carries with it the power to influence families, communities, and even broader society long after your lifetime.

Achieving this kind of wealth demands intentionality. It requires planning not only for the growth of capital but also for governance, education, and alignment among those who will inherit and manage the assets. Without this, wealth often dissipates within a generation or two, lost to mismanagement, conflict, or external pressures.

Foundations of Intergenerational Wealth

Building wealth that endures begins with establishing a strong foundation. This includes robust financial planning that addresses tax efficiency, risk management, and liquidity needs. Structuring assets through trusts, holding companies, or family offices creates legal protections and operational frameworks that facilitate smooth transitions across generations.

Education is equally vital. Preparing heirs with financial literacy, leadership skills, and shared family values creates a culture of stewardship rather than entitlement. The ultra-wealthy often invest heavily in teaching younger generations not only how to manage wealth but why it matters, instilling a sense of responsibility and purpose that anchors legacy.

Sustaining wealth across generations requires intentional governance structures that balance autonomy with accountability. Establishing family councils, advisory boards, or trusts with clear decision-making processes helps prevent disputes and ensures alignment with the original vision. These mechanisms provide frameworks for managing conflicts, setting investment policies, and adapting to changing circumstances without fracturing the legacy.

Open communication fosters unity and trust among stakeholders. Transparent discussions about expectations, responsibilities, and values build shared understanding. Regular meetings and educational sessions keep all parties engaged and informed, reducing the risk of misalignment or resentment that can erode wealth and relationships over time.

Philanthropy often becomes a central pillar in legacy building, linking financial resources with purpose. Creating foundations or donor-advised funds allows wealth to contribute to causes meaningful to you and your family. This not only amplifies impact but also instills a culture of giving that enriches both the legacy and the heirs' sense of fulfillment.

Flexibility is essential in legacy planning. Life is unpredictable, and rigid structures can become obstacles rather than safeguards. Designing adaptable frameworks that accommodate new family members, shifts in values, or evolving market conditions ensures the wealth remains relevant and effective through time. This might include periodic reviews of trusts, updating governance charters, or providing mechanisms for heirs to pursue their own visions within agreed boundaries.

Another critical aspect is succession planning. Identifying and preparing the next generation of leaders ensures continuity. This involves more than naming heirs; it requires mentorship, skill development, and opportunities for practical experience. Encouraging younger family members to engage in business operations, investment decisions, or philanthropic efforts nurtures confidence and competence.

Trusts, Foundations, and the Power of Structure

When building wealth that endures beyond an individual lifetime, the structures used to hold and manage assets become as important as the assets themselves. Trusts and foundations serve as powerful tools to preserve wealth, provide control, and create lasting impact. Far from being reserved for the ultra-rich, these vehicles offer anyone serious about legacy-building the ability to design how wealth flows, grows, and benefits future generations or causes aligned with personal values.

Understanding Trusts

A trust is a legal arrangement where one party, the grantor, transfers assets to another, the trustee, who manages those assets on behalf of designated beneficiaries. This separation of ownership and control allows for tailored management and protection of wealth according to specific terms set by the grantor.

Trusts offer multiple benefits in legacy planning. They can minimize estate taxes, protect assets from creditors or divorces, and provide for heirs who may not yet be ready to manage significant wealth. The terms can specify how and when beneficiaries receive distributions, aligning financial support with milestones or behaviors.

Beyond financial control, trusts foster privacy. Unlike wills, which become public documents upon probate, trusts remain confidential. This discretion is valued by those wishing to shield family wealth and decisions from public scrutiny or potential disputes.

There are various types of trusts to suit different goals. Revocable trusts offer flexibility, allowing the grantor to modify terms during their lifetime. Irrevocable trusts provide stronger asset protection and tax advantages but require relinquishing control. Specialized trusts can fund education, support charitable giving, or preserve family businesses.

Foundations as Legacy Vehicles

Foundations operate as nonprofit entities established to support charitable activities. They provide a structured way to direct resources toward causes important to you and your family. Foundations can range from private family foundations to donor-advised funds, each with unique legal and operational considerations.

Establishing a foundation signals a commitment to philanthropy and stewardship. It enables ongoing involvement in social impact while offering tax benefits. Foundations also engage younger generations, connecting them with values and providing opportunities to participate in meaningful decision-making.

The governance of a foundation mirrors that of a corporation or trust, with boards, committees, and formal procedures ensuring accountability and adherence to mission. This structure protects the foundation's purpose across generations and maintains alignment with evolving family priorities.

Integrating trusts and foundations into a unified legacy plan allows for both financial control and purposeful impact. For example, assets held in trusts can fund a family foundation, creating a pipeline that supports charitable initiatives while preserving wealth. This combination provides flexibility, enabling families to adjust priorities over time while maintaining structural integrity.

Effective governance is critical when managing these structures. Establishing clear roles, responsibilities, and decision-making protocols prevents conflicts and ensures continuity. Many families implement advisory councils or boards composed of family members and trusted advisors to oversee operations, set strategic direction, and mediate disputes. These bodies foster communication and shared vision, strengthening the legacy framework.

Transparency within the family enhances trust and prepares future generations for stewardship. Regular education on the purpose and function of trusts and foundations demystifies these tools and builds a sense of responsibility. Engaging heirs early promotes alignment with values and reduces the risk of mismanagement or fragmentation down the line.

Choosing the right professionals — including estate attorneys, financial planners, and philanthropic advisors — is essential. These experts bring specialized knowledge that ensures compliance with legal requirements, optimizes tax benefits, and crafts structures tailored to unique family circumstances and goals. The process is dynamic, requiring periodic reviews and updates to respond to changes in laws, family composition, or financial conditions.

While setting up trusts and foundations may seem complex or reserved for the ultra-wealthy, technology and evolving services have made access more feasible. Digital platforms offer streamlined trust administration, and donor-advised funds provide philanthropic engagement without the overhead of traditional foundations. These innovations democratize powerful legacy tools, empowering more families to build wealth that endures and makes a difference.

Teaching the Next Generation to Play the Hidden Game

Building wealth that lasts is only part of the equation. Equally important is preparing the next generation to understand, manage, and grow what they inherit. Without guidance, even the strongest financial structures can erode over time, not because of external forces but because heirs lack the mindset and skills to navigate the hidden game of wealth. Teaching this game requires more than financial literacy; it involves cultivating character, judgment, and the ability to think beyond surface-level strategies.

Moving Beyond Money Lessons

Conversations about wealth often focus on technical knowledge: budgeting, investing, taxes. While these are essential, they do not address the deeper questions of identity, responsibility, and purpose that wealth inevitably raises. For the next generation to thrive, they must first understand what wealth represents in their lives. Is it a tool for freedom? A platform for contribution? A responsibility to steward rather than spend? Helping them explore these questions early builds a foundation of meaning that outlasts any single financial lesson.

Modeling the Values Behind Wealth

Children and young adults absorb far more from observation than from lectures. The way wealth is discussed and handled within a family shapes their attitudes toward it. If they see secrecy, fear, or conflict around money, they may develop anxiety or resentment. If they witness transparency, shared goals, and thoughtful decision-making, they are more likely to adopt those behaviors themselves. Modeling gratitude, patience, and curiosity around financial choices demonstrates that wealth is not just about accumulation but about alignment with values and long-term vision.

Gradual Exposure to Responsibility

Introducing the next generation to wealth management should happen in stages, aligned with their maturity and experience. Early exposure might involve simple tasks like managing a small allowance or participating in family discussions about charitable giving. As they grow older, they can be included in more complex decisions, such as reviewing investments or contributing to family governance meetings. This gradual progression allows them to develop competence and confidence without feeling overwhelmed or entitled.

Providing real-world experiences accelerates learning far more effectively than theoretical discussions. Involving the next generation in tangible projects, such as overseeing a small investment account, participating in philanthropic initiatives, or contributing to a family business venture, gives them a sense of ownership and direct feedback on their decisions. Mistakes become valuable teaching moments rather than failures to be avoided, building resilience and critical thinking that no classroom can replicate.

Mentorship plays a vital role in this process. While parents and close relatives provide foundational guidance, exposure to outside mentors broadens perspective and reduces potential bias. Trusted advisors, entrepreneurs, and professionals can offer insights that complement family teachings, reinforcing lessons while challenging assumptions. These relationships also introduce future leaders to networks that will prove essential as they begin to navigate their own financial paths.

Formalizing education through family meetings or retreats creates consistency and structure. These gatherings serve as opportunities to review goals, share updates on family enterprises or investments, and reaffirm shared values. They also provide space for open dialogue, allowing younger members to voice questions and ideas. Over time, such practices normalize financial discussions and prevent the secrecy that often leads to misunderstandings or conflict later on.

Encouraging personal vision within the context of family wealth is equally important. While shared goals provide unity, each individual must also feel empowered to pursue their own passions. Supporting entrepreneurial ventures, academic pursuits, or creative projects helps the next generation see wealth as a tool for self-expression rather than a constraint. This balance fosters independence and innovation while maintaining respect for the larger legacy.

Ultimately, teaching the hidden game is about transferring more than financial acumen. It is about instilling a sense of stewardship, humility, and adaptability that enables future generations to thrive in a complex world. When they understand both the mechanics and the meaning of wealth, they are equipped not only to preserve it but to expand its impact, ensuring that the family legacy remains vibrant and relevant for decades to come.

Chapter 12: Living Beyond the Secret

When Money Stops Being the Goal

For many, the pursuit of wealth begins with a desire for security. Covering basic needs, eliminating debt, and building a safety net provide relief from daily stress. As wealth grows, the goals often shift toward freedom: the ability to choose where to live, how to spend time, and who to spend it with. Yet for those who reach significant financial success, there comes a point where money itself ceases to be the primary driver. At this stage, the question is no longer "How much is enough?" but "What now?"

The Diminishing Returns of More

Psychological research consistently shows that beyond a certain threshold, additional income has little effect on day-to-day happiness. Studies by Nobel laureates Daniel Kahneman and Angus Deaton, for example, highlight that once basic comfort and autonomy are secured, emotional well-being plateaus. For high achievers, accumulating more money does not necessarily solve deeper questions about meaning or fulfillment.

This realization often arrives gradually. The thrill of hitting financial milestones fades more quickly than expected. Possessions that once symbolized success lose their luster, and the chase for bigger numbers begins to feel hollow. The absence of external pressure to earn can also uncover internal restlessness, forcing a reevaluation of what truly matters.

Redefining Success Beyond Numbers

When money stops being the central aim, success is measured differently. Instead of net worth, it may be defined by impact, freedom of choice, or personal growth. This shift does not negate financial goals but places them within a broader vision. Wealth becomes a tool rather than the destination — a means to create, contribute, and explore rather than merely accumulate.

For many, this phase invites deeper questions about legacy. How can resources be used to shape the lives of loved ones, support causes that matter, or solve problems larger than oneself? The answers vary, but the common thread is that fulfillment stems less from what wealth provides for the self and more from what it enables for others.

Navigating this transition begins with understanding personal drivers that extend beyond financial gain. Many discover that true satisfaction comes from mastery, creativity, or contribution rather than accumulation. Engaging in projects that challenge the mind, expand skills, or positively affect others transforms the relationship with work and wealth. The energy once directed solely toward earning shifts toward building something enduring or meaningful.

Purpose-driven goals often emerge during this phase. Philanthropy becomes more than an obligation; it turns into a way to align resources with values and create measurable change. Supporting education, funding research, or investing in community development allows wealth to serve as a catalyst for solving problems rather than merely signaling status. For some, this leads to the establishment of foundations or impact funds that continue to operate long after they step back from active involvement.

The psychological shift can be profound. Without the pursuit of more as the central motivator, some feel unmoored, unsure of how to measure progress. Reframing success in terms of relationships, health, and personal growth requires conscious effort and reflection. This process often leads to a simpler but richer life, where experiences and connections take precedence over acquisition.

Practical adjustments also support this new phase. Rebalancing investments toward stability, ensuring estate plans are in place, and setting clear philanthropic strategies free mental space for new pursuits. Instead of obsessing over markets or returns, energy can focus on mentoring, creative expression, or building meaningful ventures that align with personal vision.

The Ethics of Hidden Knowledge

Wealth is often built not just on hard work but on information and strategies that are not widely understood. The concept of "hidden knowledge" raises an important ethical question: when you know something others do not, how should you use it? Throughout history, this tension has shaped not only fortunes but also societies. Elite networks, trade secrets, and advanced financial strategies have given some individuals and families enormous advantages, often creating divisions between those with access and those without. Understanding the ethics of this dynamic is essential for anyone seeking to use knowledge responsibly while building lasting success.

Knowledge as Power and Responsibility

Hidden knowledge is powerful precisely because it is scarce. Whether it involves understanding tax law intricacies, anticipating market shifts, or mastering negotiation tactics, insights that remain out of reach for most people can create disproportionate results. But with that power comes responsibility. When used ethically, hidden knowledge allows innovators and leaders to create value, solve problems, and elevate others. When misused, it can reinforce inequality, exploit vulnerabilities, and erode trust. The ethical dimension lies not in possessing the knowledge itself but in the choices made with it. Information asymmetry is inevitable in complex systems; no one can know everything. What matters is whether the application of that knowledge benefits only the individual or also contributes to broader well-being.

Transparency vs. Secrecy

A key tension in the ethics of hidden knowledge is deciding when to share and when to withhold. Total transparency may seem virtuous but is not always practical or even safe. Releasing certain financial strategies or proprietary innovations prematurely can undermine their effectiveness or allow competitors to exploit them. At the same time, hoarding information for personal gain without regard for consequences can perpetuate harm.
Navigating this balance requires discernment. Ethical stewards of wealth often choose selective transparency: sharing insights that empower others without compromising security or the integrity of their strategies. This

might mean mentoring, teaching principles rather than formulas, or funding education and research rather than simply guarding resources.

The Moral Weight of Advantage

Possessing hidden knowledge can create an internal moral challenge. Does benefiting from what others do not know make the success less legitimate? Should those who understand the "rules behind the rules" feel obligated to level the playing field? History shows a spectrum of responses. Some elites have used their advantages solely for personal gain, while others have built institutions, funded social programs, or shared frameworks that allow others to rise.

Applying hidden knowledge ethically begins with intention. The first question to ask is whether using this information creates value or merely extracts it. Strategies that exploit loopholes or prey on others' ignorance may generate short-term gains but often lead to long-term harm, both reputational and societal. In contrast, approaches that transform insight into innovation or improve systems create benefits that extend beyond personal profit. This shift in mindset reframes wealth from being a private game to being part of a larger ecosystem.

Practical frameworks help navigate the gray areas. One approach is to evaluate impact across three dimensions: personal, relational, and societal. At the personal level, ask if the strategy aligns with your core values. Relationally, consider whether its use fosters trust or erodes it with partners, clients, or communities. Societally, reflect on whether the outcome contributes to fairness or exacerbates systemic imbalance. These questions do not always yield easy answers, but they provide clarity in moments where purely financial calculations fall short.

Mentorship and education are powerful ways to balance advantage with contribution. Sharing principles, mindsets, and ethical decision-making processes empowers others without necessarily revealing every detail of a strategy. This approach builds capacity rather than dependency, helping others develop their own insights rather than simply relying on inherited secrets. Families who embrace this philosophy often create generational cultures of stewardship, where each member feels both privileged and responsible for the knowledge they inherit.

Another key element is legacy. Hidden knowledge is often most impactful when embedded in structures that outlast the individual. Trusts, foundations, and educational initiatives can carry forward insights and values in ways that continue to shape future generations and communities. This ensures that the benefits of specialized knowledge are not hoarded or lost but transformed into enduring contributions.

Ultimately, the ethics of hidden knowledge rest on the awareness that access itself is a privilege. Choosing to wield that privilege with integrity transforms the pursuit of wealth into something more profound: a path to influence that uplifts rather than isolates, and that turns personal advantage into collective possibility. By treating hidden knowledge as both a gift and a responsibility, you position yourself not just to play the game at a higher level but to redefine the game for those who follow.

Creating Your Own Playbook

Hidden wealth strategies and insights are valuable, but their power is magnified when transformed into a personalized framework. Every individual faces unique circumstances — different goals, risk tolerances, timelines, and values. A personal playbook ensures that the knowledge you acquire is not just understood but applied in a way that aligns with your life, creating a repeatable system for decision-making and growth. Without such a framework, it is easy to fall into the trap of chasing trends or copying others without understanding whether those approaches truly fit your situation.

Defining Core Objectives

The foundation of a personal playbook begins with clarity of purpose. What are you building wealth for? Is it freedom from financial anxiety, the ability to create opportunities for your family, or the pursuit of influence and impact? Many never pause to answer this question, and as a result, their strategies remain scattered. Defining core objectives creates a lens through which all decisions can be filtered. If a potential move does not serve your larger aim, it can be discarded regardless of how attractive it might seem in the moment.

Clarity also prevents comparison with others. Wealth strategies that work for someone aiming to retire early may not suit someone focused on building a multigenerational enterprise. Understanding your own endgame ensures that you are not borrowing someone else's definition of success.

Identifying Strategic Advantages

Every individual has access to certain strengths or opportunities that can be leveraged for disproportionate results. This might be specialized knowledge from a profession, access to a particular network, or the ability to take calculated risks that others avoid. Mapping these advantages helps you design strategies where you have an edge rather than competing where you are weakest.

This self-inventory should be brutally honest. Recognize areas where you lack expertise or discipline as well. A strong playbook does not pretend weaknesses do not exist; it builds systems to mitigate them, whether through partnerships, advisors, or structures that limit exposure to avoidable risks.

Crafting Guiding Principles

A playbook is not just about tactics; it is also about principles. These are the rules you will not break even when opportunities seem tempting. Principles might include commitments to ethical wealth-building, long-term thinking, or maintaining specific boundaries around lifestyle inflation. They function as anchors during turbulent times, keeping decisions consistent with your larger vision.

Translating guiding principles into action requires designing a system that is both structured and adaptable. This begins by outlining specific financial strategies that serve your defined objectives. For some, this may involve prioritizing cash-flow assets like rental properties or dividend-paying stocks to ensure steady income. For others, the focus may be on growth vehicles such as private equity or emerging industries that offer higher potential returns but require longer horizons and more risk tolerance. The key is alignment: every asset and every decision should serve the ultimate purpose you clarified earlier.

Decision-making frameworks add another layer of strength to your playbook. These frameworks help you evaluate opportunities consistently rather than react impulsively to external noise or short-term trends. One approach is to establish clear criteria for any new investment: required return thresholds, acceptable levels of risk, alignment with long-term goals, and potential impact on liquidity. By committing to objective evaluation, you avoid the emotional swings that lead many investors astray and maintain a disciplined approach even during periods of volatility.

Regular review processes ensure your playbook evolves as life changes. Quarterly or annual assessments allow you to measure progress, identify weaknesses, and adjust course without losing sight of your larger vision. These reviews should go beyond financial performance to include qualitative factors: Are your actions still aligned with your values? Has your definition of success shifted? Are there emerging opportunities or threats that require rethinking the structure of your plan?

Building a playbook also means creating mechanisms for feedback and learning. Documenting decisions — why they were made, what assumptions were present, and what outcomes resulted — turns experience into a continuous source of refinement. Over time, this record becomes invaluable, allowing you to recognize patterns, avoid repeating mistakes, and sharpen your intuition for future moves.

Finally, integrating accountability strengthens the entire system. Whether through mentors, peer groups, or advisors, having others review your plans and challenge your thinking reduces blind spots and reinforces discipline. Wealth-building is rarely a solitary pursuit; those who succeed most consistently are those who invite honest input and remain humble enough to adapt when better information emerges.

A personal playbook is not a static document but a living framework. It evolves with your circumstances and deepens as your understanding grows. By designing it around clear objectives, leveraging personal strengths, embedding ethical principles, and committing to regular reflection, you create more than a strategy for financial success. You build a compass that guides every major decision, enabling you to navigate complexity with clarity and transform knowledge into enduring advantage.

Last Words: Thank You

If you've reached this page, it means you've done something few people ever do: you've taken the time to question the narratives you were given about money, power, and freedom. You've looked beneath the surface to see how the game is really played — and more importantly, you've chosen to step into that game with awareness rather than blindly following someone else's rules.

The insights you've just read are not meant to stay on these pages. They are tools, perspectives, and frameworks you can return to as your life evolves. Wealth, in its truest sense, is not static. It grows with you. It deepens as you learn, as you fail, as you succeed, and as you redefine what "enough" really means.

Thank you for trusting me to guide you through this journey. My hope is that this book becomes more than information — that it becomes a quiet companion in the moments you feel lost, a challenge in the moments you feel complacent, and a reminder that you have more power to shape your reality than you were ever told.

Carry these lessons forward. Pass them on to those who need them. And never forget: the hidden side of wealth was never about money alone. It was about unlocking the freedom to live fully, to create boldly, and to leave behind something that outlasts you.